COME WALK THE WORLD

THE COURAGE TO RISK
Traveling With the "Greatest Generation"

Malcolm Eudaley

authorHOUSE®

AuthorHouse™
1663 Liberty Drive
Bloomington, IN 47403
www.authorhouse.com
Phone: 1-800-839-8640

© 2009 Malcolm Eudaley. All rights reserved.

No part of this book may be reproduced, stored in a retrieval system, or transmitted by any means without the written permission of the author.

First published by AuthorHouse 10/12/2009

ISBN: 978-1-4490-2240-2 (e)
ISBN: 978-1-4490-2239-6 (sc)

Library of Congress Control Number: 2009908880

Printed in the United States of America
Bloomington, Indiana

This book is printed on acid-free paper.

DEDICATION

To my wife of sixty three years
Evelyn Lucille Baldwin Eudaley
Artist, Teacher, and Companion
As well as our three daughters
Linda Walker
Janice Eudaley
And Elizabeth Diddle
Our Two Son-in-Laws
Two Granddaughters
And Two Great Grandsons

Also
To the Thousands of People
Met in my travels who reside in Metropolitans as well as
Those existing at the Edge of the Earth.
Still eating from Clay Pots,
Some of whom you will meet
In the pages of this Book.

And To You;
Have a good Life.

TABLE OF CONTENTS

DEDICATION	V
INTRODUCTION	IX
IT BEGAN VERY SIMPLE	XI
GLOBAL EXPOSURE	XV
CHAPTER 1 MAKING AN ENTRANCE	1
CHAPTER 2 YOUNG YEARS IN TEXAS	11
CHAPTER 3 MULTIPLE WORLDS IN VIEW	17
CHAPTER 4 NAVY DAYS	24
CHAPTER 5 BACK HOME	44
CHAPTER 6 WALKING ON WATER	55
CHAPTER 7 A NEW BASE	76
CHAPTER 8 ENTREPRENEUR DAYS	102
CHAPTER 9 THE FAR EAST	141
CHAPTER 10 LATIN AMERICA	151
CHAPTER 11 GLOBAL EXPOSURE IN THE WEST	162

INTRODUCTION

The challenge presented in this book will encourage you to step into the water, even though you will never walk on it. Some books become masterpieces of fresh insight. Other books teach on great subjects, while others inspire and motivate an isolated person in some far corner of the earth on any Continent.

Seeds were planted to write in a hotel room one night in Guatemala. Later, encouragement continued to rise as my wife and I were in conversation with our three daughters. The decision was made.

I was fortunate to have been born during the 'greatest generation'. We were presented a world in conflict. Tom Brokaw wrote about such a world. Simply stated, that world no longer exists. We were not a perfect generation, but we possessed a deep seated quality and respect for life. We knew at least something about

Economics 101. Morals and ethics were more defined. Language was more civil. We could communicate without using crude language, at least in the presence of ladies. Neighborhoods were more cohesive. The places of worship were highly respected.

A journey it would be and the walk was begun. Beginning days are shared in order to set the story in motion. The travel covers 32 years in 50 nations, meeting with hundreds of people from different cultures who found and lived out their faith against all odds. They, like us, are strangers and pilgrims on this planet. There are no permanent nesting places here. Movement is ongoing. So, Come Walk The World with Me.

Malcolm Eudaley

IT BEGAN VERY SIMPLE

The distribution of time and space for my life has been from a farm in a wagon to NASA where men/women live on a space station. Life has flowed from the simplicity of the past into a very complex and high tech world. The majority of people in my beginning years lived in poverty. Toys were rare possessions. I recall begging Thomas Kyle, a friend of mine in grade school, for a chance to ride his bicycle since I never owned one.

The memory of our going to church in a wagon is fresh in my mind. Returning home one night a major rain storm happened. It probably took 45 minutes to make this trip to our house. Now, NASA can have a space ship in orbit in 8 minutes or more. It is much quicker than we could make the trip home that night.

Day old bread was 5 cents a loaf. It was common for a man to earn a dollar a day. Seeing a doctor was a rare experience for us. Often a medicine show appeared in our little town. A couple would park on a vacant lot and set up a small platform on the back of their vehicle. One of them would do a little entertaining and then the sale of their medicine would begin. The promises made for this fake medicine would bring about a cure for any health problem. This so called medicine had High Alcohol content. If this medicine did not take care of your illness, at least it made you happy.

In the summer when school was out our Mother would prepare a good lunch for us. When we completed our meal she would insist that we wash the dishes. Then we could go to the Brazos River to swim. Our learning to swim class was different than the present. The young boys would be picked up by the larger boys and thrown into the deep water. We quickly learned the art of swimming. The 4th of July was spent on the beach of the Gulf of Mexico. Fish would be caught in a huge 300' long net. Here I met Crabs, Flounder, Trout and Sand Fiddlers.

Flounder and Trout were special foods for us. The Gulf of Mexico also challenged us with dangerous under tows and powerful waves. We survived against all odds. The real test for survival was to come later. Such challenge would continue to come, but through different venues as we processed Life.

Global Exposure

A sweeping invitation at the beginning of this journey is for you to travel with me, as well as a host of people, either on a bus or train or ship or plane. In fact, we will be in a wagon, a cart and other strange vehicles. Lots of walking will also take place with a little snow in Alaska at 35 below zero and a trip into Northeast Russia on Aeroflot. We will enter the city of Khadbarovsk. It is full of unfinished buildings due to a major financial cut back by Moscow.

The pastor we are visiting will take us to a funeral. The deceased is a poor peasant woman who lived in a high rise on the third floor. Millions of these poorly constructed buildings exist in the old Soviet Union. Her viewing is in the parking lot of her building. There are two saw horses where her simple casket is set. Her few friends walk by. There is no black Cadillac Hearse present. Her trip to the cemetery will be on a rough, flatbed truck. We will walk with her to one of the most rugged places of burial to be seen in the world.

Our journey will take us east and west, north and south, and around the world.

Our goal is to observe and hopefully inspire and strengthen you, as well as to expand the concept of having a Christian Worldview that impacts our thinking and our involvement.

The exceptions will be Africa and Australia.

Through the entire journey there will be rivulets of stories along with some philosophy of life. I have been a pastor as well as an entrepreneur on a spiritual journey. On these walks we will enter different cultures. The motivation is not for financial gain. In fact we have been able to share over $400,000 for projects supports as well as strengthening teachers, schools, pastors, and erecting buildings, as well as share medicines for children. A faithful donor base made these efforts a reality.

The U.S. is not the largest, nor necessarily the most beautiful place on the planet. The rest of the world is much larger than we think. It has its share of beauty. The people are different. They adapt and relate to their cultures - the only one they know. Yet, there is a great similarity of what the human face is about. We do have strong similarities since we are all creatures created in the image of God. Even Gorbachev thinks Noah actually had an Ark. So God must exist after all, if He says so.

These people, who make up families on the earth, are struggling to survive. I met a lady in the Philippines one day. Her husband was away doing his best to catch fish. A friend asks her about the future. She did not know what the word 'future' meant. When asked about the day, she responded by saying "she hoped her husband would come home tonight and that he would bring food for a meal." There were four children and an infant living in her house on Stilts. A vast part of the world is in a simple survival mode while we, in most instances, expect to be successful and as well as healthy.

We will mix a little history and a lot of story telling about the areas that we have visited and the experience we have had. The beginning will be from the days of the great depression of 1929 and onward. As the trip expands we will enter China, Malaysia, Cambodia, Philippines, Eastern Europe, Russia, Ukraine, Latin America, and the Caribbean. Many of these people we will see are the poor of the earth. They live in ghettos or cardboard cities in the regions mentioned above. The places they live are tough, dirty and mean. Many still live in the country struggling to raise food stuffs in order to have something to eat.

One of the highest honors I experienced was to travel to these nations and met so many amazing people of faith. Wonderful contacts became available along with good translators on these journeys. To be in their homes, eat with them, sleep in their beds, hear their stories and sense what it was like to live 24/7 in their village, town or city became experiences which are never to be forgotten.

A short account of our life starts the journey, but the Big Story is the people who have embraced the Christian faith in places where oppression and poverty are in power. Often these encounters confirmed that "the last shall be first."

CHAPTER 1
MAKING AN ENTRANCE

My trip began when my mother said to my Dad and the family - (three children already) "Well, it is time." I had no voice in the matter. I appeared on the scene in 1923. It was on a Wednesday, October 17th. I have no idea if the sun was shinning or if it was raining and cold. There I was. That was 86 years ago. Again, I am at the place where I have little to do or to say. Very seldom do I have a speaking platform, so I have decided to write. Wander with me through the thousands of days that I have lived. Some of the days I crawled, some I walked, some I ran, many I flew. Come, let's take the Walk.

Decade one and two allowed me to finish High School in 1941. I really enjoyed these two decades. This was followed by three years at sea in the Navy. I have never walked on water, but for three years I lived on water. The sea was good and bad. Often it went wild. Other times it was as smooth as glass with flying fish racing with us alongside our bow. These were good days.

Bad days followed. At the close of an invasion we would be standing along side the dead and the wounded. These were Soldiers or Marines who had died on the beaches and were returned to our ship for burial at sea. Later our own crew would die in fire and shrapnel. I was beginning to see the reality of life and death at the age of twenty.

There is nothing like "TAPS" being blown on a bugle or trumpet as your close friends slide off into the ocean. There is no marker for the grave. Only the latitude and the longitude were recorded in the Ship's Log. The military also fires a few rounds from a rifle to close the service.

When my day ends... Please no rifles.
Just Taps, played by a good trumpet man.

In the world of the Navy the best for 'recreation' was a can of Beer. When we dropped anchor off some island, probably in a deep cove, we would have 'recreation time' on a sandy beach. Three cans/bottles of beer would be passed out to us. The Chaplain was in charge. I took the beer and sold it for $1/bottle. I never was around a Minister who pushed beer. Yet, on Sunday I would go to Chapel and hear this fellow preach. Why? I suppose it was because my Mother took me to church as a kid. Bad as I was, I still went to church.

Only one time did I hear a Chaplain speak with clarity. The Marines were landing on the beach the next morning and this Baptist Chaplain presented something worth hearing, especially to young men that might die. It was at the invasion of the Marshall Islands. Some did die.

Nothing happened for me in these Chapel services each Sunday. However, I have always thought if I could have nine lives, like the proverbial cat, I would like to be a Navy Chaplain in one of those lives.

STILL WALKING

I was home again in 1946 with a marriage to follow. I met and knew Evelyn Baldwin for three months. We are still together 63 years later and still in love. I told her that yesterday. Four years later I received my degree at the University of Oklahoma. A short stint in business ended with a brief career at General

Motors in Kansas City. Twenty-two years followed serving as a pastor. From there to a new beginning, serving on the staff of World Vision International, one of the world's largest relief and development Agencies.

Later I traveled as a Christian entrepreneur visiting nations where we associated with small bands of Christians who rose above the governmental restrictions that existed in their situations. They also rose above their cultures where many gods were in place. We will visit some of these strong people of faith.

At retirement, I, along with a selected Board of Christians created a 501© non-profit Corporation. Out of this creation multiple trips were made to conduct Pastor Conferences along with assisting Christian Schools with textbooks, teacher conference support and some new school houses. To visit with Christians all over the world helps one to know how "big" the Kingdom of God is that stretches around the world.

NAILING IT DOWN

Everybody has a story. Remember, though, few want to hear your tale. On one of my many trips into Latin America, a friend of mine, who is the Latin American Director of the Association of Christian Schools, Dr. Stuart Salazar, shared with me in a hotel room in Guatemala a simple statement. "Malcolm, you ought to write a book." My response to him was that I was to busy living life to stop and write about it.

MIND CHANGE

I changed my mind about writing.

It was a little village near Paris, Arkansas. The days were rough. Dad did a little coal mining and later a little farming. His Dad had owned a small general store in the country. Some years ago I visited with a cousin of mine and she had in her possession a small ledger book. My grandfather, whom I never met, had written in this little book the names of his customers and the items they had purchased - a nickel here and 15 cents there - a pinch of salt and a pound of sugar. The astonishing thing as I viewed his book was his perfect hand writing. That I did not inherit.

Out of this rugged setting my mother chose to visit a church. There she listened to a presentation of the Christian faith. She embraced the Gospel. Mother did not have a formal education. If she had had the opportunity of some of us, she would have earned a Master's degree. She now has five grand children who have their Master's degrees.

Her days were the late 1800's to the mid 1900's. During her life some had the privilege of attending school, but not many. I never looked on my mother as an unlearned person. She had a strong sense of purpose for herself and her children. There was a dignity and strength about her that gave her a desire to pursue life with vigor. This made the difference in her family. Though she missed the opportunity of a good education, she gave to her children a sense of being and purpose. She passed it on to us.

At that time my mother and a lady by the name of Kenny Nichols decided to begin a Sunday School. A small community opened their arms to these two ladies. After several months my mother shared with Mrs. Nichols that she was pregnant again with her fourth child. I was that child. Soon their activity came to a close. I was 32 years old before she shared this story with me. Later I will share with you why she kept this secret to herself for all those years.

I think there must have been a depression where we lived a long time before the crash of 1929. People were moving about the country hoping for better things, like bread on the table. Some went off to California, the land of milk and honey. Now in 2009, many are moving back to their old settings. Why not, when a simple little house on the West Coast can cost a quarter of a million dollars or more?

Others were making decisions to relocate in other lands of opportunity. Mr. Woods, my mother's father, decided to relocate in south Texas. Stories of some prosperity were coming out of a place called Freeport, Texas, located south of Houston on the Gulf coast. There a company was mining sulfur and the pay was good. He made the trip and began to encourage his married children to come to this land. Three of his children, including my Dad and Mother, made the move. Reality brings about change in ones life.

It was years later that I genuinely came to appreciate my Father. Dad was indeed a common man. I doubt seriously that he ever recovered from the effects of the depression. He was always cautious in his decision making. His jobs were very menial. Stepping out into some business venture was not for him. Dad worked in a custodial job. My brother, Gervis, later became a successful Contractor with Dow Chemical Co. He was in Dad's building one day and met the Executive of that division.

When the Executive discovered that they were father and son, he shared with Gervis his high regard and respect for our Father. Dad was a good man with an excellent reputation. The decision our father made to move the family to Texas eventually proved to be one of his best and wisest choices.

A STORY OF MY DAD'S

When he was a boy of ten or twelve his father took him to a County Fair. When they arrived he was surprised by a scene that he came upon. A man had dug out a smooth deep hole just the size of a barrel. He had taken the ends out of the barrel. The barrel was placed in the hole strapped securely to the ground. A special harness was designed that would be used to secure himself in the barrel.

Everyone arrived at the Fair Grounds in a wagon or buggy pulled by a team of horses or mules. The Fellow would challenge these Farmers to pull him out of the barrel. When he found a challenger, he would put on his harness, get into the barrel, pressing himself against the inside walls. The farmer would then connect his team to the harness and urge his team to pull.

Farmer after farmer had paid his fee hoping to be the winner of the pull. The horses would try, then let up and pull again, never successful. They only had a few minutes to empty the barrel of this well secured man. A fellow with a team of mules took a look at this proposition. He took the challenge and was set to pull. First there was no movement. Then the mules got serious. They went to their knees. Dirt and rocks were flying. The man in the barrel comes out. Years later I would tell Congregations this story and follow up with "The Man at Midnight" (Luke 11:5-13) along with the "Widow before the Judge," (Luke 18:1-8) Dad taught me an excellent lesson in persistence!

When I was 10, the pastor of the church that we attended was named Sanders. It was a small group without much potential or so it seemed. In spite of this insignificant happening, Pastor Sanders made an impression on me that affected my view of life. Each Wednesday morning he would begin a walk to the Texas Clemens Prison Farm. It was a huge facility where black Americans prisoners were committed for their crimes.

Pastor Sanders did not own a car. He would leave Freeport headed west, across the Brazos River bridge, on past Gulf Park and Jones

Creek, arriving at the Prison Farm. There he was allowed to speak to some of these men. Week after week he made this journey to meet with these *forsaken Men*. He was persistent in his task. The faithfulness of this man in a world that hardly knew he existed was a testimony to me - a lesson in persistence.

Hope someone got the lesson then. I think I did.

The amazing Teacher, Jesus, is still attempting to speak through his stories of old. Don't let anyone TEMPT you with the foolish notion that the things he taught are not relevant today! He is far more relevant than some College classes or Textbooks. A niece of mine enrolled in a sociology class at the University of Houston. The first statement made by the professor was, "If any of you profess to be Christian, I promise you that I will shed you of your faith by the end of this Semester." Tolerance had gone on a long journey that day. Intolerance had taken up residence in the mind of a supposedly educated man.

CHAPTER 2
YOUNG YEARS IN TEXAS

On the trip to Texas we traveled in a Model T Ford. I think it was a 27-28 Model. Dad had sold everything to buy the car. We had our clothes and possibly a few pots and pans. Upon arrival we settled into a $10 month rental house. It was hard to imagine that we could have been happy in such a place, but we were - five children in a two bedroom house. Dad searched for work. We children started to school. We were on a "roll" buying day old bread for a nickel and off to Sunday School in clean clothes, scrubbed on a washboard.

School began in Velasco, Texas. Things were going great. We had settled in this little town of 300 people located across the Brazos River from Freeport, TX. Freeport was a more affluent town of 3000 people. Later we moved to Freeport where life took on a better look. There I finished high school.

Mom began the search for a Church. The family would be connected to a life of faith. Life was no hit or miss proposition for her. When she entered the 'walk of faith', she set her sights on establishing a set of values that she understood from studying our Lord's life. Her Christian value system had convictions. Later in her life when one of her boys decided he would challenge her position, she stood her ground. My brother brought home a six-pack of bottled beer and placed it in her refrigerator. He laid down to rest in a bedroom. While he was asleep, she took the six-pack to our backyard and smashed every bottle.

SEGREGATION AND HURRICANES

Long before Martin Luther King, my mother taught us about "racism." She met and developed a relationship with Aunt Ida Jammer along with others in her community. Aunt Ida was a devote Christian as well as a Deaconess in the Methodist Church. She also was a Black American. While I was still in high school Aunt Ida would come by to visit with Mother. My brother Paul would be present and Aunt Ida would say to him, 'Paul, when are you going to become a Christian and preach the Gospel?" She got us boys mixed up it seemed. While I was in the Pacific during WWII, Aunt Ida passed away. The church she attended invited my Mother to share about their relationship as fellow Christians at her funeral. Our family was so pleased for this invitation. A large group of Black American women also attended our Mother's funeral.

When I was nine years of age our brother Tommy died from an accident following the 1932 hurricane that hit the Gulf Coast. Its force was wind. He was working on a clean-up team in Freeport. A rusty nail pierced his shoe. He was unaware that he needed a Tetanus shot. He was dead 3 days later in our hospital. Tommy and I were very, very close.

In 1934 another hurricane came in from the Gulf of Mexico. Our small village was just four feet above sea level. This storm's force was water. We were four miles from the beach front. The water traveled at full force into Velasco, approximately 3 to 4 feet in depth. One block from our house a neighbor had built his home high enough to keep the water from entering. Our father asked for permission to bring his family to this house for safety. It did not happen. Later we will talk about who our neighbors are in this Life.

Malcolm Eudaley

THE CHOICES WE MAKE EVEN IMPACT KIDS

I entered grade school in Velasco. There I encountered a lady that would become my second grade teacher. The community expected teachers to have strong ethics and good morals. Such people had a value system based on an active faith. The culture was more Christian at this time. Maria Dykes, my teacher, was a role model even at this early age. We children looked to her as an important figure in our lives.

Miss Dykes was dating two men. On a select day a fellow whose name I don't remember would come after school to drive her home. He owned a taxicab service and most of the community thought he was a 'bootlegger'. The next day Bob Evans, the Sinclair agent, would come. We kids began to pull for Bob Evans. Already there had been instilled in our little second grade minds that there was such a thing as right and wrong. Bob won the lady in marriage and we children were happy over the wise choice of our teacher.

It has been my privilege to have a life long friendship with her nephew, Bob Girouard. We finished high school together. Later we joined the Navy together. On a vacation trip to Texas, I met one of Marie Evans sons and shared my love and respect for his mother and how she had touched my life.

HIGH SCHOOL

High school was a very positive experience. Even in those depression days we had a caste system in place. There were people who lived very comfortably. The Executives at Freeport Sulphur Company led the way. Pilots who served incoming and out-going ships that docked in our harbor were successful. My best friend's father owned the Girouard Grocery. It was a forerunner of the coming Super Markets of today. Bobby and I cleaned and dressed chickens each Saturday. Our pay was 10 cents per hour for 10 hours.

It never occurred to me that my family was poor. I knew we were, but it never weighed heavy on my psychic that one person was better than another person simply because one owned the house he lived in. School was a happy place. Miss Rahl and Miss Jordan were fine ladies who attempted to teach us Literature and English. God bless Miss Jordan. Jerry Bryant was our Band Director. Mr. Gore, the Principal knew how to use a paddle and often did. Coach Hooper shaped up the football team for each season.

Malcolm Eudaley

One year I showed up for spring football practice weighing in at mighty 115 pounds. I dressed for practice. If I recall I made it for one afternoon after two guys ran me down with my nose in the turf. There were some great stars on our team. Well, it appeared they were the greatest to the Exporters fans. For me golf became my favorite sport. Our town had a nine-hole golf course. The Greens were grass. There were no sand traps, nor hills to climb; just flat Texas land with a great Club House build by the Sulphur Company. Caddy fees were 25 cents a round. Eighteen holes produced 50 cents. This amazing money made it possible for me to buy my clothes for high school. Willard Wood, who is my cousin, played a lot of golf on this course. He was good on the fairways and I was fair on the greens. He became a professional and followed golf as a career. His son, Willie played golf on the PGA tours.

CHAPTER 3
MULTIPLE WORLDS IN VIEW

Why would anyone ever attempt to put into writing a book after turning eighty six?

I suppose there could be several reasons.

-Reflecting over 8 decades plus - could be good for the soul.

-For sure there are some things that need not be told.

However, in looking back it is good to be able to say that most of what I have experienced has been good. Yes, there are regrets in select decades, but it is good to be here and forgiven. WWII allowed me to grow up fast. I prefer "not to study war no more." Yet, I chose to share some of those stories.

Not everyone has the privilege to see the world as the Navy says. But if so, let that person share what the globe has exposed to him/her.

The stories are about real people - people at home and around the globe.

The University also impacted me. At 30, I left the business world and entered into the world of becoming a people person. I have not seen it all. I have seen more than I ever dreamed I would see. For 20 plus years people went into hiding when they discovered I was a Minister. Immediately they would clean up their language and put on a new face. So look for a little of my philosophy of life. The Christian Worldview is also included. You have to close the door on the past before the door to the future can be opened. That door opened for me. Hopefully it has opened for you.

ENJOY!

What a privilege to have graduated from a University being a farmer's son. Spending 20 plus years as a Pastor I discovered the difference between Reality and Fantasy. There is so much Fantasy. Thank God, there is also some Reality.

Experiencing 'global exposure' has opened up a whole new understanding in my life. Being escorted into a Ghetto by two policemen in Guatemala to visit a school is an eye opener to another world. I confess I am not a tourist.

Some sites are great, but very little is just there to be seen. Travel, at its best, should have purpose: from the Opera House in Kiev, Ukraine to a Symphony Hall in Warsaw, Poland. To receive the most out of travel your focus must be on people. You learn from people.

Concentration camps are not for tourists. They are the toughest places. Dr. Viktor Frankl is the author of a book entitled *Man's Search for Meaning.* He writes of those who manage and control Concentration Camps. There is no harder assignment. As a prisoner, Frankl shares the many choices that prisoners make. Some give into circumstances. Some commit suicide. Others chose to live against all odds. He concludes his book by saying, "We have come to know Man as he really is. After all, Man is that being who has invented the gas chambers of Auschwitz. He is also that being who has entered those gas chambers upright with the Lord's Prayer on his lips.

Such a person entered the Gas Chamber knowing who he is. It is important to know who we are. Many do not know which way is true North? They do not know the Principles to follow, and who to follow. Are we to base our lives on a shallow concept of being? Are we living a secular life denying the existence of who we are? Does our life-style tell the real story of who we are? Can we recognize and see the true mean of Life? Are we off balance not anchored to a true value system?

It is good to discover what is important in life without being imprisoned. 9/11 should have helped us. Frankl also states "When we are no longer able to change a situation, we are challenged to change ourselves."

City Dwellers may have a difficult time understanding Eugene Peterson in The Message. Peterson translates the writing of a man named Habakkuk. Modern man knows what it is to have the stock market collapse; bonds down in value and unemployment increasing, but does he know there is something more significant about life than Property and Positions. Man, indeed has a Soul.

Habakkuk, speaking to an agrarian population says:

"Though the cherry trees don't blossom and the strawberries don't ripen,

Though the apples are worm eaten and the wheat fields are stunted,

Though the sheep pens are sheep-less and the cattle barns empty,

I'm singing a joyful praise to God. I'm turning cartwheels of joy to my Savior God.

I'm counting on God's rule to prevail; I take heart and gain strength.

I run like a deer. I feel like I'm king of the mountain."

FREE IN THE TWENTY FIRST CENTURY?

Not really.

There are KGB Agents, Russian Czars, US Politicians, U.S. Czars, and Executives serving in glass boxes in the corner office. Often Professors in America's Universities are pushing their own agenda upon young, immature adults. People warehoused in systems of bondage. Cultist schemes are present throughout the Earth. Others cannot leave their settings having been cloned by Corporations, Institutions, Churches, Unions and Political Parties. Free, I wonder.

Yet there are others, like the residents of a Presbyterian Leper Colony in Thailand, who are free! We discovered a 'Band of Christians' taking communion in a shell of a Theatre in the Ukraine. It was the Common Cup with half of those present, sick in the dead of winter. We will meet Bernie, a Baptist pastor on the Island of Palawan in the Philippines washing the feet of some strangers. Victor is a transit Carpenter in the Ukraine who is a Bio-vocational Preacher of the Gospel. The KGB was present. They were not free. Victor is free. The vast majority of those living in this land were not free.

LET'S WALK
THE WORLD

Through Villages, Town, Cities across oceans, on trains and ships, in the air, on boats...

East and west, north and south, cold and hot,

Good beds and bad, driving with a horn, packed in like sardines,

Good people, bad people, some saints and some sinners, even a 'con artist', a pretender, little people, great people, and good food, bad food.

Seldom a good hotel, often a bad flight, luggage lost for days, standing in the rain, 35 below zero, a beautiful world, a hurting world.

The smell is different, the food strange. Don't drink the water, protect your Passport.

Be careful with the exchange of money. Keep an eye on your luggage. Adapt to the culture. Travel light. Somebody will speak English.

Every body has a beginning and an end.

We all hope we will be fulfilled with a happy day.

Hopefully your beginning will lead you on a quest to find Reality.

All the beginnings for people who live on this earth begin sometime, somewhere. The choice of where we begin is not of our choosing. In fact, a great deal of life evolves without our having input. When you look back on your 'launching pad' you were placed there by One who knows all about you. You were first in your Mother's Womb. It was a very ideal and safe place to begin this life. It is not such a safe place today. When the journey is over and the departure time comes, strange thing, you will not have input at departure time. Your seat on that final flight will be an 'assigned seat'. Have a good Trip.

CHAPTER 4
NAVY DAYS
───────────

Decades last only so long. The first two were slipping away quickly. Grade school and high school were major times of learning and adjusting. The Big Event was just around the corner. For a year I worked in the Dow Chemical Plants, but something was about to happen that would shock the entire world into a kind of Reality we knew nothing about. We would be entering World War II. I would be going as a young sailor into the U.S. Navy. This was the beginning of my seeing lands I never dreamed of and meeting people of many cultures.

The Navy met me in Houston, Texas. I was sent to San Diego on December 1, 1942. After 'Boot Camp' I returned to Houston. Then we are on our way to New York City. A small town boy on Times Square didn't seem quite real. The people treated us like royalty. Pepsi gave us drinks and a hamburger for a dime. The

Navy was bringing together a crew for a new ship being built in the Brooklyn Navy Yard. Production was delayed and so I remained in the city for four months. Our quarters were at Pier 92. It had been remodeled for a Navy barracks. There was really nothing for us to do but wait for the U.S.S. DuPage to be commissioned. What an experience. My assignment was to clean up the "Officers Bar" each morning. This was the closest time for me to eventually becoming a bartender. It was a soft job. I have never tender Bar since those days.

Four months in the Big Apple was quite an experience. There was Radio City Music Hall where every Big Band in existence would appear for a week or so. If I recall service men were allowed to attend on a 25 cent ticket. The Bands of Glenn Miller, Tommy Dorsey, Jimmy Dorsey, Harry James, Guy Lombardo came and many others. This was the day when music had some quality.

At the Community Club house in Freeport we had the music of these Big Bands. Oh, some of the music was a little crazy, but it kept many of us out of trouble. Some of those favorites are still in my head and once in awhile I get them out and stir up old memories.

While I was in New York I recall taking a young lady to see a movie at the Astor Theatre. It was a film of Mickey Rooney's called *The Human Comedy*. The story line was about the war. Mickey and hundreds more were on a Troop Train moving across the country. Each soldier was a little sad since he was leaving for some destination not of his liking. Mickey got out his guitar and asked the fellows to join him in a song. Mickey suggested that they sing "Leaning." Since no one in the group knew the melody he begins to sing.

"What a fellowship, what a joy divine

Leaning on the Everlasting arms."

He goes on to the chorus and finishes singing,

"Leaning, leaning, leaning on the Everlasting Arms."

I was not a Christian at that time, but I sure understood what Mickey was singing about. In fact, I never embraced the Christian faith until I returned home from the Navy.

While in NYC at Pier 92 either the Queen Mary or the Queen Elizabeth would tie up at the adjoining dock each week. When I begin to serve as a full time Pastor, the memory of this experience surfaced in my mind. The challenge to put this story into print surfaced. The story of these two ships and their service to the war effort developed as a "conclusion" to one of my sermons. It is the story of what happened in many lives of people and institutions. So many of us have had *great dreams,* yet they were allowed to die.

In the summer of 1943 thousands of soldiers would come to New York City. Grand Central Station was often packed with these men. They were to board either the Queen Mary or the Queen Elizabeth headed for England. These luxury liners were owned by the British. The war was picking up in fervor. Preparations for "D" Day were in full swing. Thousands of troops were needed for the invasion of Europe. Tons of food and supplies were loaded along with the equipment needed by these men.

The turn around of these ships was fast. After they were loaded, tug boats would come and nudge the Queens out into the Hudson River. The tugs would guide them just so far, then they would pass the Statue of Liberty and in less than four days, depending on the weather conditions, they would be crossing the Atlantic to England - back and forth - week after week.

A war was on. It called for wartime sacrifice. Men in Army fatigues were eating out of metal trays where there had once been china, silver, crystal and linens. Ladies had been dressed in lovely gowns, men in black ties and everyone living in comfort in exquisite state rooms. Military men headed to war. Men slept in 8-tier bunks. Comfort was set aside. The affluent surrendered their privileges. The survival and hope of a continent was at stake. The peace of the world hinged on these actions. People would suffer. Almost 300,000 U.S. servicemen would die. However, there was a commitment in these difficult days. I doubt that there has been such a commitment since those days? The nation could well have lost this kind of strength and loyalty. Has the Culture moved so far to the left that our eyes are being blinded to the Christian Judeo ethic? Are we people of strong character with dignity and significance as our goal in the pursuit of Life?

THE QUEEN MARY AND HER FINAL DAYS

These are very sad days for the Queen. Many of you would know that she no longer travels the sea lanes. Possibly you have visited her. She is tied up at dock side in Long Beach, California.

She is a museum now. No longer in service. No longer in action.

There is no Captain on her bridge.

No well-disciplined crew on board.

No passengers of pleasure or well-trained men for battle.

People come to visit her. I went to see her.

There was something very sad about it all.

There is no fire in her boilers.

The soul of her is gone. No anticipation for the sea.

No real life. The Queen is Dead in the water.

Ships are created for the open sea, but all she is doing is

Entertaining at dock side on a make believe journey.

There is nothing like a ship at sea with a set destination

The Navigation comes from a fixed object, such as The North Star.

There is fire in her boiler. She is going somewhere.

There is nothing like a Nation, or a Church, alive, on course, with a

Captain at the Helm, fulfilling the task for being.

A redeeming force in action, lifting a broken world;

It is exhilarating to be on such a journey.

A good Crew on Board is important.

Sometimes I wonder if some Institutions, some Churches

are tied up in a lot of activity, dock side, with plenty of

Entertainment, even thinking they are on a great journey,

A kind of Fantasy, with no Reality.

The story of the Queen Mary is an amazing account of what has happened in the life of many people and institutions. So many of us have had great dreams, yet they were allowed to die. A Pastor of a Church I attended one Sunday in Los Angles shared these thoughts.

- Some people have simply stopped expecting, having lost hope.
- They have accumulated enough of life's disappointments.
- Afraid to dream, to reach, to stretch, to broaden their horizons.
- But God wants to free us for our tomorrows.
- He won't allow us to blame yesterday.
- Neither will He allow us to cast blame on anything or anybody who seems to have restricted our living.
- So we live to 70-80 and beyond, but in actuality, we may die at 50.
- Causius Clay once stated, "If you are the same man you were at 30 as you now are at 50, what a waste."

FROM NEW YORK CITY TO JAPAN

After the commissioning of the DuPage we went on a 'shake down' cruise. Then we were off to Norfolk, Virginia. Cape Hatteras was next with the Panama Canal ahead. From Hatteras to the Panama Canal, sea sickness was my lot. It is no exaggeration that sea sickness brings on a wish for death.

Passing through the Canal we entered the Pacific, we encountered ground swells 30 to 40 feet in height. If there was ever a testing of how a ship had been built, it was in these waves. Our bow was forty feet in height. When waves reach that high everything that will shake loose will shake loose. In this environment the ocean is challenging the ship and the crew for their right to be on the sea. A wave would lift us at mid-ship, leaving the bow and the stern with no ocean under them for support. The ship would have its beam tested, every rivet, every weld tested to the limits. We made it through, arriving in San Diego.

Now we are on our way to Seattle and a return trip to San Diego. Next would be Pearl Harbor. The Marshall Islands was our first invasion. The Marines won. We went back to Pearl Harbor - loading again and on to Guam. From Guam we invaded the island of Peleliu; one of the most horrible places where so many Marines died. Next it was Guadalcanal. We went to New Caledonia to get a camouflage paint job on the DuPage. New Caledonia was governed and controlled by France. What a dirty place. For Christmas of 1944 we headed back northwest to New Guinea.

SAILOR MEETS A LADY

Something different and very special happened as we dropped anchor off the New Guinea coast line. A signal was received by our ship asking if a Malcolm Eudaley was on board. Our signal bridge answered affirmative. The message had been sent from an Army Nurse named Doreen Powell. Doreen was from Freeport. Her sister Vivian had dated my brother Tommy years before.

Our crew had not seen a woman after many months at sea. The ship went wild. A second message arrived with an invitation for me to come ashore to visit with Doreen and spend the night. The Executive officer gave me permission to go to the beach for this visit. Doreen met me at the dock and we spent a leisurely afternoon and evening together. Chow with the Army was not that great. I now knew why I had joined the Navy. Later a place was arranged for me to sleep in a tent for the night. A big mistake was about to happen. I failed to tuck the mosquito net under my mattress. That night very hungry mosquitoes got to me. They were almost as big as the Texas variety I had known in my youth. The next morning I told Doreen goodbye and headed back to the ship.

Ten days later on December 25, 1944 - Christmas Day - I was standing on deck listening to an army orchestra that had been invited aboard to entertain the crew. A great lunch was served for them and us. In return they gave us the best of the music of Glenn Miller along with Tommy Dorsey and Harry James and other bands. The same music I loved in high school. I still love the sound. As I was standing on deck listening to this great music I suddenly turned into a "wet noodle," wilted and fell unconscious. It was Malaria. The 'sick bay' personnel rushed me to the medical facility where I spent four days totally out of touch with reality along with several more days in recovery.

ACROSS THE PACIFIC

Late in December of 1944, after Christmas a fleet of ships prepared to depart from Hollandia, New Guinea to invade the island of Leyete, on the southern tip of the Philippines. There is an estimated 7000 Islands in this Nation. The recovery; from malaria was slow. My weight had dropped to 110 pounds. Most of the action was light compared to former battles. The serious part of that invasion was taking place at sea off the northeast coast of the Philippines. Carriers, battleship, destroyers, cruisers were fighting the Japanese Navy. A second trip was made to Leyete with more troops.

We then begin preparation for the invasion of Luzon off the Northwest coast of the Philippines. Fifteen attack transports along with support ships (destroyers, cruisers, etc.) entered the Lingayen Gulf. This very large body of water connected with the South China Sea. The invasion was not contested in a major way by the Japanese. Yet men died. It was a major event for some.

THE NIGHT THE WHEELS CAME OFF - KAMAKIZE TIME IN THE PHILIPPINES

It was January 9, 1945. The troops had made their landing on the beach near San Fabian with little opposition. The fight was to begin later as they marched to Manila. On January 10th, our convoy got under way to return to New Guinea. It was dusk as we steamed out of the Lingayen Gulf. As we were leaving the Gulf there appeared two Japanese twin engine bombers coming in from the northwest. The entire fleet began to fire at them with our 5:38 guns as well as our twenty mm guns. The shells used in the 5:38 guns weighed 54 pounds. We had no luck at shooting these two aircraft down.

Suddenly one of these bombers turned back to the China Sea. The other continued to fly south toward Manila. They were gone, we thought. The one that turned back to the China Sea eventually dropping his altitude, flying very low, and returned just twenty feet over the water. This Kamikaze pilot planned to sink our ship.

When he came into view he simply pulled back on the stick in order to clear our forty foot bow. The plane struck our port side at mid-ship. All hell seemed close!! The plane was destroyed, plowing through the super structure. Fires were burning. Steel was twisted. Twenty MM guns were damaged. A large bomb lay on the deck that had failed to explode. Thirty-three men were dead. Dozens were injured. Shrapnel was everywhere. Many were burned. Four men picked up the bomb and dropped it overboard. The wheels of the Kamakize plane came off. The entire plane was destroyed with the pilot killed. His grave is in the Lingayen Gulf today. By morning 36 of our crew were dead. January 10, 1945 lies deep in my memory.

LOST AT SEA

There was no damage to the starboard side of the ship. For those of you who are not familiar with sea language, that is the right side of the ship. All of the guns on the ship were manned. A crew of three to four men manned this twenty mm anti-aircraft gun. When they saw the fires burning out of control on the port side, they became so frightened, they jumped overboard. The gun captain tried to restrain them but with no success.

We were sailing in three rows of ships with five in a row. Orders were quickly given to the four ships following us to change course so that these sailors would not be in the path of the ships that followed. That night the Navy did something we had never seen before. Our Flag Ship Admiral ordered destroyers and destroyer escort ships to make a search for these men. They turned on their 24 inch search lights to scan the waves. As these waves of light penetrated the darkness these men would raise themselves as high as possible out of the Waters. They were lost and they wanted to be found and rescued.

On occasion I have shared this story of these three frightened men jumping into the ocean. The search lights began to scan the waters. This always brought to my mind how desperate people become when they wonder if they will survive. There is a strong desire to live in all of us. We want to live. We want to be found if we are lost. A child lost in the woods wants to be found and so does a man, especially when he senses a nearness to the end of his life.

Three of the greatest stories you will ever read are told by The Man – yet more than a Man. The stories are simple. The first is about a lost sheep. The second is about a lost coin. Then third is the classic story of a lost boy. (Luke 15) M. Neilson states that no word ever spoken by Christ is or ever will become obsolete. The Word 'Lost' is still a significant word, no matter how sophisticated we become. The three men who jumped into the ocean were so glad the Navy cared enough to rescue them. There was a good man on the bridge that night.

I BELIEVE IN MIRACLES

After the Kamakize attack, several member of the crew who had been injured were transferred to the U.S.S. Merigold, a hospital ship. Thirty six men were killed in action that night. Fifty three of us were wounded and received a Purple Heart. We were on our way back to New Guinea. Of all things, we would be interned in an Army Hospital. After several weeks of being treated for burns, a transport that was in harbor in New Guinea prepared to leave for Pearl Harbor. I do not remember the name of this ship, but it was British. A small number of us were on board. The days were momentous. Providentially I picked up a copy of TIME magazine that I found on board. It had no advertisements in it. Also, it was about half the size of the normal state-side publication. I read it through.

When I came to the health section of the magazine there was a story about two army doctors who had served in the Pacific. They were stateside doing research on Malaria. The results were that when a service person returned from the Pacific who had experiences malaria and had taken the treatment they prescribed, he/she would have an 85% chance of never having malaria again. I will ever be thankful to these Doctors and to TIME for publishing this information.

Their findings discovered that a Malaria victim, if he would take an 'Atibrim pill' three times a day for one week, he would have a good chance of never experiencing Malaria again. I immediately went to the ships Medical Office and ask if he had 21 Atibrim pills in his pharmacy. I showed him the article and he gave me the pills. I took this medication gladly. The result was that the surface of my skin turned a very brilliant yellow in color. I looked terrible. But as of this day in late Fall of 2009, Malaria has never come near my door. Anyone who has had malaria would consider this a Miracle.

When we arrived in Pearl Harbor we were transferred to another vessel and sailed for San Francisco. The DuPage was in port being repaired. A thirty day leave was granted to all of us upon our arrival in San Francisco. I was back in Freeport for thirty day. It must have been a shock for my parents to see me in get off the Bus as a yellow man.

JAPAN WAS STILL ON THE HORIZON

The days were still uncertain since the Japanese had not surrendered. When the crew regrouped in Frisco our ship was assigned to take an invasion force for the attack on Japan. Troops boarded with all their gear. Again, we sailed under the Golden Gate Bridge. That day flashes into my memory even now. It was chilly with overcast skies. There was no sunshine. A mist was in the air. Lonesome and tired of war we settled in for a long journey to Japan.

Most of us were in our early twenties. Everything was on hold for our future. We were tired of war - men like George Blanchard, Elwood Conway, Muscatelli, DuPont and two sailors named Cobb. We were assigned to the Gunnery Division. This trip for us was of no interest to us. No one had the slightest idea of what was before us. And then it happened. Japan surrendered on August 6, 1945.

ANCHORS DRAGING

When we arrived in Japan we were delayed in entering Nagoya, our port of call. Due to that delay the ship pulled into a cove south of Nagoya. We dropped our starboard anchor for the night. Since the crew was not privy to information being gathered on the Bridge for the Captain, we settled in for a quiet rainy night. It was not to be. A typhoon blew into the cove. The wind gathered its forces and our ship began to drift toward the shore. The Captain ordered the port anchor to be dropped. Yet we continued to drift. The storm was increasing in its fury.

With power ready in the engine room, the Captain ordered that we move 1/3rd ahead.

We stabilized with both anchors out and the Propeller turning. We had power in our boilers. The Bridge ordered that we continue with the bow into the wind. As the propeller begins to turn, the ship was brought under control, but not moving. It was holding its own in the storm. There was some fear present, even among the 'old salts'.

Some days we needed all the anchors we can find. For sure we needed a source of strength to supply us with moral power. If we chose to use short-term selfish interest and refused to sacrifice for long term results, we will pay the fiddler of triviality. When people have established a Christian Worldview they discover a source of power in the Trinity that will enable them to ride out the storms.

Soon we were on our way to deliver the troops. They would be some of the first to occupy this broken nation. Seldom were we ever in a port where we tied up to a dock. In Nagoya docks were available for us.

The Executive Officer announced on the PA system that there was to be no liberty for the crew. We could not believe him. When dark came, with the ship tight against the dock, the crew made up of over 500 sailors left the ship by the dozens, if not hundreds. We slipped over the lines going ashore to see the Japanese people. They treated us with great respect. We carried cartons of cigarettes with us and used them for bartering since we possessed none of their money.

The ultimate collapse of Japan had become a reality with the dropping of the two unbelievably, powerful bombs. The great debate of Harry Truman's decision goes on. We did not debate this issue. Thousands of young men would not be making this invasion. Every branch of the Military had experienced serious loss. All of the Armed Forces had experienced fires, death, and destruction. We were glad to go Home.

CHAPTER 5
BACK HOME

The Navy Days were over on January 6, 1946. I started for home. Have you ever gone back to something that would never be the same for you? You thought it would be as it always was, but the place had changed. The people were okay but something had happened to you on the inside that would take you to another place. It was not that you felt a kind of superiority, that you were better than the family or the surroundings. It was just over for you. Many of my friends remained and spent their lives in the old familiar surroundings. It would always be their home. Life was good for them.

Years later on a visit my friend Bob Girouard said to me, "I just cannot image that you left Texas. And to think you enrolled and graduated from the University Of Oklahoma.

For him, this was an unforgiveable choice I made. We are still the greatest of friends.

It took awhile to sink in. It also happened that I was the only one of my many family members to who left south Texas. Cousins, nephews, nieces, most of them remained in Texas. Several trips have been made to visit the place again. My father and mother remained until they slipped up to the gate of death and into another life. They went to a place where the King lives. Two brothers and a sister have also made their exits. Gervis and I are the only remaining members of the clan. We are close. Gervis had an amazing conversion at West End Baptist Church. He has a great heart. He and Glenda had three children, two daughters and a son. Steve, their son is deceased.

Paul, my oldest living brother was a maverick through and through. Often in our young years we clashed. He was independent in his choices and thinking. He was a tradesman – a hoisting engineer, a self-made man. Fishing and hunting were his passions. Gervis and I have shared with each other that there would never be as many people at our funeral as were at Paul's. The chapel was full. His family asked me to speak. To this day I remember some of the words that were used. "Clocks do stop and Dust always settles, but the human spirit lives on." Paul and Hazel had three sons; Durwood, John Paul and Harvey Joe. Harvey Joes is deceased.

Gladys was my sister. She was the oldest child and was married to Dolph Wood. Sis had two children, Tommy and Kaye. She was a very private lady who lived with a great deal of pain. She was a dear sister, who, on one occasion gave me a great gift that I so appreciated.

MAKING THE TIE

Before leaving the salt grass prairie of south Texas a good friend of mine did me a favor. He had a sister living in Kansas City where most of his family lived. While on vacation in KC he convinced her to come with him and his wife to Freeport. Evelyn had spent the war years working at a Defense Plant that produced B-25 Bombers.

I had no idea of what was about to happen. Here comes this beautiful 22 year old into my life. Our first date was a trip to the Gulf of Mexico on Surfside Beach. She had never seen the ocean. Setting on the jetty with her was an exhilarating experience. Her golden hair was free, blowing in a soft breeze. I remember how she was dressed; A beautiful grey suit with a lovely soft, thin black blouse. Not to revealing, just right for a classy lady. She was and is still a great lady who knows how to put things together. She is a good mother, an artist, a decorator, a writer, an excellent cook and an outstanding teacher. Her oil paintings are displayed throughout our home. On February 23, 2010 we will have been married sixty-four years.

OFF TO COLLEGE

The G.I. educational benefits that were provided for all veterans of WW II were waiting for me. Evelyn resigned from her job at Southwestern Bell in Freeport. I worked a short time with a survey crew out of City Hall. Our next stop was Oklahoma City where we began our educational experience. Later a transfer was made to the University of Oklahoma.

My first two years of college were at a private Christian school now knows as Southern Nazarene University. During these days I had been working toward a degree in Business. I was also processing a decision as to whether I should enter the Ministry. A decision was made to move to the University of Oklahoma. I finished there with a B.S. in Business in 1950.

An opportunity opened for us in Kansas City. Yet, I continued to search for my place in life. When I resolved this, I enrolled at the Nazarene Theological Seminary in KC. At the same time I accepted a job assignment with General Motors. After my Seminary training a resignation was given to GM and we were off to experience the best of life for us. Two children had arrived in the family prior to this move.

Our first daughter arrived while we were in our first year of college. Years later Linda completed her college work and eventually finished her Master's Degree program at Drury University in Springfield, MO. She has completed thirty years as a school teacher. An attempt was made by Gene and Linda to adopt a Chinese baby through a contact I had in Malaysia. The child was born with a heart defect and the adoption was closed. It is very tough on our psych to let it be known that we are old enough to have a retired child. Linda resides in Springfield, MO with her husband Gene.

Janice, our second daughter was born while we lived in Kansas City in the 50's. She completed her college degree at MNU in Olathe,

KS and has her Master's Degree from the University of Missouri Kansas City. She now serves as the Coordinator of Student Enrollment at a Community College in St. Louis, MO.

Elizabeth is our third daughter. She has her degree as well as her Masters from Kansas University. She is on staff at the downtown Children's Mercy Hospital of Kansas City. She is involved in Hematology/Oncology Social Work. Elizabeth and Brian Diddle have two grown daughters who have their degrees. Sarah and her husband Aaron have a son named Lincoln. Brian and Elizabeth's second child is Emily. She is graduating in 2009 from Azusa University in California.

When a couple speaks of their children they have to be very careful. It is such a natural thing to overstate their achievements. One of the most dangerous things about life is to possess an over abundance of pride. There can and should be a healthy pride. But a pride that is full of a foolish arrogance makes everyone sick except the person who has it. Hopefully I speak with a well-earned pride about our daughters and their families.

In the late 90's I needed to make a trip into Lebanon. My friends, Bob and Norma Brunson, met me at the Beirut Airport. I was scheduled to visit a school in this city as well as two schools in Jordan. Beirut had experienced several years of conflict between two factions. After making our visits and later flying to Amman, Jordan, to visit two schools, we were in conversation about Families and Life.

My friend Norma simply stated, "There are no families that are not dysfunctional." In reflecting over the many encounters with people of all descriptions, rich and poor, educated and uneducated, black or white, Asian or European, if you go deep enough into the roots of the family trees you will find something dysfunctional. Regrettably, a degree in higher education does not change people as it relates to bias and prejudice. Often you will find that the people who call for tolerance are the most intolerant with those who do not agree with them.

Dr. E. Stanley Jones, a great writer and speaker who served at least 40 years in India as a Methodist Missionary, tells a story of speaking to a Civic Club in a Southern State. He made a simple statement that could have turned the meeting into a riot. He said: "If you have a little "kink" in your hair, you might have a little black in your blood." WOW!!

When I was a young boy I had a lot of "kink" in my hair. Be cautious about bragging. You probably will eat your words. Remember, we all came from the First Adam.

ROMANIA MUDDY RIVER BAPTISM
Roses were not present at this event

UKRAINE PASTOR TRAINING EVENT
The Church never died under Communism

TATINA, A RUSSIAN SCHOOL PRINCIPAL
A Force for Good in Russia

Come Walk The World

LENIN and EUDALEY
Lenin still stands in most Cities

THE CHINESE GATHER FOR CHURCH
Possibly the Strongest Church on the Planet

CRUISE SHIP or RIVER BOAT
Charles Baldwin, the Professor on a River Cruise

ELSA, A GUATEMALA SCHOOL PRINCIPAL
A Nation Blessed by Strong Leadership

CHILDREN WITH NEW TEXTBOOKS FOR THE YEAR IN GUATEMALA

PARAGUAY TEACHER EXTENSION EDUCATION

CHAPTER 6
WALKING ON WATER

BECOMING A PASTOR

Often, as ones enters a new environment, people experience great change. A new life opens up. Evelyn and I had gone through a major flood in Kansas City. That was in 1951. Our apartment was under water up to the ceiling. The only things to be salvaged were dishes, pots and pans and silverware. An opportunity to buy a new home surfaced for us. Simple as it was, the thoughts of leaving it was difficult, more so for Evelyn than me. But a new world was before us. Little did we realize what this world would provide for us?

The real lessons, beyond the world of books, begin when you assume a leadership role, be it business, government or an institution. You will soon discover what you are made of, especially when you get up on a Sunday morning at 6 am, go into the basement of a struggling little church, to build a roaring fire in an old furnace that should never had had another fire in it. The fuel supply was wood cut by members in the Ozark hills. We had entered the world of being a Pastor. An amazing life evolved as we became closely connected to those we served.

Once we were ready to leave Kansas City we were offered a pulpit in Mountain Grove, MO. The church was located 60 miles east of Springfield, MO. It was a small town of 3,000 people. It had one small manufacturing plant - a shoe factory. A very picturesque square was in the center of the downtown business section; probably 30-40 businesses.

The church was only a mission outpost located in an old Funeral Home. The building must have been 80 years old. It was located on the center of three city lots across the street from the Public School. It was an excellent location. A small apartment was set up in the rear of the building. The chapel seated 72 people. The congregation was made up of about 30 people - a few children, probably 6 young people and maybe 20 adults. Twelve of the adults were 60 or older. The salary was

$35 per week. General Motors was some what better. Here, it was like "walking on water."

After a year the chapel was full with 60-70 or so people. A discussion began regarding erection of a new building. The place was coming alive. People were happy. Our Board started the discussions. One very good man opposed this project. He was the most influential person on the Board. His position in the community was that of a High School teacher. It was great to see him move forward and see the project completed.

Our prosperity here was not in money, but in finding a group of people who knew who they were and were devoted to seeing something good happen. We arrived with a '51 Chevrolet paid for and $300 in our pockets. There was no health care in the package. This little congregation began to show their "love" by providing us with things like milk, eggs, apples from an orchard, meat (prime beef) and vegetables. They accepted us. Our two older daughters to this day look on this place with strong positive memories.

When I was in the business world one of my assignment was to make professional calls on Architects and Engineers. We needed such men to guide us through this building program. They were not present. However, plans were developed and we began to schedule our construction. First, this small group gave $1,500 to begin. Our next step was to visit Mr. Duval, our local Banker. We ask for $4,000. Mr. Duval was a Baptist. Later he shared with his Baptist brother-in-law that if we defaulted he would turn the building into an apartment house. There was no General Contractor on site.

The building was started. A small man in body, Scott Ham, showed up on the first morning. He was probably 70 years of age. There was a beautiful, cherry tree standing in the center of the site where we would build. This good man brought a cross-cut saw for us to use in cutting the tree down. I was 31 years old at the time. My friend worked me into exhaustion before the tree fell.

The footings were dug with shovels. The concrete was mixed on site and poured. A sub-floor was laid. Walls went up. Mr. Sullivan, a Baptist friend who was about 80, appeared one morning to help us. His hands were gnarled and crippled with arthritis. He simply said to me, "Preacher, do you need a little help?" As I looked at him, I thought what could this good man do for us in his condition. The construction crew consisted of four old men and a young preacher who had never built a chicken coop or a dog house. How could I have known what was in store for us?

One Monday morning a local Pastor drove up and saw me driving nails. He kindly dressed me down for doing such common labor. I simply said to him, "I am probably making more friends doing this than I made yesterday morning in the pulpit." We preachers and our church might be more respected if we entered into the real world with our people.

In this little town there was a fellow that everyone knew as Ralph. Ralph was a little mentally deficient. Winter and summer he wore a long Army overcoat that almost touched the ground. One day at a Ministerial Alliance meeting we talked about Ralph and his visits to our churches. He moved from church to church. I wondered if Ralph had not been sent to our churches. By his visits, possibly the Lord could check us out to see if He could bless us. He would have a hard time with a group that was proud. It is important that such an individual be welcomed in any church.

The morning we were prepared to cut the rafters Mr. Sullivan saved the day. He told us just how to make the cuts on the rafters. I suggested we put up the first set of rafters to see if they fit. These special ordered rafters were so expensive that I wanted to be sure. He affirmed everything would be alright. They fit.

By this time Mr. Sullivan and I were good friends. In conversation one day I told Mr. Sullivan that he could tell his brother-in-law, Mr. Duval, that he would never be able to foreclose on this building. Fifty-eight year later, after all of those years, this building remained as a place of worship. Two other buildings were erected on this site before we moved on to another assignment – a two-story educational structure and a nice, new parsonage.

The secret that my Mother kept to herself since my conception was revealed to me by her in a letter at this time. She shared this after my being in the ministry for two years. It was the simple statement Kenny Nichols made about my future on their way to the little rural Sunday School when my mother was expectant with me. The statement was "that I, the infant, could become a minister end even touch the world." Little did I know the direction I would travel?

In 2008 I was invited back to preach the 'last' Sunday morning worship service in this Chapel. In attendance that day, were grandparents, their children and their grandchildren; People who had become Converts to the Christian faith when Evelyn and I was their Pastor.

Today there stand on a six acre tract in this city a new $600,000 sanctuary along with classrooms. The building is an excellent structure. Dr. J. K. Warrick was invited to speak at the dedication of this new building. Was this ever a day of confirmation! There is some irony, for me, in the way life unfolded here. A competitive bank purchased the former site and erected a beautiful building. To see the church make money off of a bank was wonderful.

Many changes have been made from 1954 to 2009; some for the good and some not so good. One thing has not changed, nor will it ever. People still have the Good News shared with them. The one person of the ages, He is the same. He is still addressing the issues of our lives. The Big Picture is here to see. It is no small thing when He addresses us in the dark night of the soul. He is still saying "I still love the world and you."

There are dozens of stories from this experience yet to be told - Archie Irvin, over 70, nailing on shingles - Charlie Dowden, a man whose wife had deserted him, yet still remained true to his faith. There was Betty Taylor and her sister Ruth who bought all the shingles for that first building. They purchased this roof from Montgomery Ward on credit. The Tool sisters, Mildred and Maxine, served in our educational program for children. Herb and Mary Ann Frazee kept us in fresh Black Angus beef. Eldon Duey, who was converted one night, servicing a car in his auto service shop. Two young boys who attended our Sunday School classes now have their PhD's. Both of them came from very poor backgrounds. On and on it could go.

It is so good to find your place – to engage life with purpose. For me it was moving from a world of fantasy to a world of reality. My world is not your world, but there is a place for you.

In the first church we served, we discovered great souls who were strong in their faith. Often we set at their tables and had superb meals and fellowship. People were coming to faith. The church grew from 30 to 110 in those days. To serve them was better than being President of the local Bank whose only goal was to make money.

Pastor Adam Parish is the current minister of this church. It is so good to see young men come forward and keep sharing the Good News. It is much better than the news you read in Newsweek or The New York Times or hear on Fox News.

THE NEW MEETS THE OLD – OUR SECOND CHURCH

In a sense people are the same everywhere. To a degree that is true. Yet, there are differences that exist in some settings. For sure any 20-year old is different than a 60-year old. After six and a half years in our first church we made a move to our second church. This church was located in Neodesha, Kansas.

It was well established in the community. A new, lovely building had just been completed under the excellent leadership of a friend of mine, Wendell Paris. Internally it had reached a zenith of accomplishment. There were established patterns of practice. People were in place. Why change? Eventually every church develops a personality all its own.

Then there appears a new person – a pastor – who has arrived with a pattern of leadership that was a little different from past men who had served them. I had just come out of a developing situation that was on the move. Three buildings built in 5 years. New people were being added to the church.

Some wonderful things developed in this four year event. We had some converts to Christianity. To this day I have good memories of some of these people. Margaret Lewis came into the group as well as other. Margaret was struggling with a habit that she wanted to break. Through prayer, wise thinking and exercising patience and discipline, she won the battle.

FORTY YEARS LATER – TWO LETTERS FROM THE PAST

Forty years is a long time. Evelyn and I later moved back to Kansas City. The computer age was in full swing and we secured our Gateway. Through long struggles it became a wonderful way to communicate, especially with the email as a new way to connect with friends as well as a great tool for overseas work.

One day as I opened my computer and was surprised to receive an email from one of the family members who had attended this second church. The letter was from Elaine Sannes, a young teen-ager who attended the Neodesha Church. She told me of her conversion to

Christ while we were the pastor of this church. She was at a youth camp for her group and I was the speaker for the day. There she became a Christian.

Later, possibly a week, another email letter appeared. This letter was from Linda Baldwin, another young teen-ager from Neodesha. She shared with me that she had become a Christian while we were her pastor. I remember that Linda had beautiful red hair. I was amazed to hear her story. Often a pastor wonders just how much is being received by people who listen to him preach. I was not sure Linda was listening. I was wrong. In her letter she shared about her journey. After securing her education she had moved to New York City and lived for a period of time working in her profession. Later she moved to Dallas and there met a young man who was established in his career. He became a Christian. He and Linda later married and now serve as a Pastor of a Baptist church located in Canada.

After receiving these two letters, I resolved that I would never again try to judge or decide for myself just what the results were in any given situation. Only God knows how effective a person has been in a given time frame of life. There are stories like Jonah. He decided he was not the man for Nineveh. How wrong he was. Even Moses looked on himself as being inadequate for his task.

Some body believes in you, even if you look like a failure to yourself. Accept the fact, even if it is only your mother who believes in you.

MOVING TO THE CITY – THE THIRD CHURCH

Springfield, MO was beginning to expand and grow in 1964. Known as the Queen city of the Ozarks, she was becoming a population center for southwest Missouri and northern Arkansas. Today it serves a wide, expansive market, possibly close to a million. The Scenic Drive church extended to us an invitation to become their Pastor. Scenic Drive was located on the west side of town. An old frame building had been moved to this site and was being used as a place of worship. It was a pathetic structure due to its age and its being moved 20 city blocks.

A new, beautiful red brick building was under construction on the site when we arrived. Building programs are usually difficult, however this one developed in a very successful way. Our 'time frame' at this church was almost seven years in length. An educational building was added along with the development of the entire front of one block for parking.

With these new buildings Scenic Drive was ready for growth. Occasionally our attendance would hit the 200 mark, averaging 153 or so. This was a strong group of people who were well established in their desires to grow and serve. Outstanding laymen/laywomen were faithful to the body. Everything came together that was attractive to new people. It was the first church that we served where some very poor people as well as some very successful people worshipped. Some were owners of strong companies while others made their way by punching a time card. I thank God for these days where serving a cross section of people came together.

Many people entered the Kingdom of God here. In my reflections it would not be possible to cover all the stories but here are two. Bill Schultz was a guard at the Federal Medical Prison located in Springfield. One day he asked if I would like to visit the prison. I agreed and the event came together. While visiting a select prisoner the man asked me if I knew Dr. Paul Rees. I told him that I had met him. The prisoner began telling me a story of his childhood. He had lived in a given city where Dr. Rees' father was the pastor. He stated that he had played with Paul when they were boys. As the conversation processed I shared with him that he was very fortunate to know this family. Later, I would meet Dr. Rees and tell him of my meeting with this man in prison. As our visit came to a close, I asked if we could have prayer together. He was very receptive. I don't know if this man experienced an encounter with the Lord. I pray he did. When Bill and I left the prison, Bill said to me that he wanted to become a Christian. He accepted the amazing offer of God to man and became a follower of Christ.

The second encounter that I remember was with Willard Pierce. He and his family would attend a Sunday School class, but would leave after the class was over and go directly to one of the major lakes south of Springfield. This was their life-style pattern even before we arrived as pastor. It remained their pattern after we arrived. Willard had an excellent position with one of the best Corporations in the city. Then something happened – first to me and second to Willard.

Dean Baldwin, by brother-in-law and District Superintendent of this region phoned and asked if I would like to go to the President's Prayer Breakfast in Washington D.C. I was surprised, yet for some unknown reason,

I questioned whether I should go. On Sunday evening I phoned and told him I didn't think I could go. The next morning he and a friend were off to Washington.

On Thursday of that week, before I could have returned from D.C., another phone call came about noon. It was Willard Pierce. He asked if I could see him that day. He shared that he would be driving to his home for lunch and asked if I would come to see him. When I arrived Willard immediately began to tell me what was going on in his life. He began by saying that he was under some kind of cloud. He also shared that in his sleep at night, he was having dreams or visions of some of the people who attended our church. He said they were praying for him. Then he asked, "What is happening to me?" I simply told him that I thought that he was experiencing the same thing that all people experiencing when they discover their great spiritual need. The salvation extended to all people through the cross and the resurrection of Jesus Christ, was available to everyone, including him. I mentioned his need to pray. He said, "I don't know how to pray." We knelt to pray and he asked that I lead him into prayer. The first words Willard said after he repeated the prayer were, "The load is gone from me."

Willard was in church the next Sunday. He shared publicly of his discovery of faith and his sensing that he had been forgiven of his past. He began to purchase Christian books and Bible commentaries for study. Today he is holding steady, living the Christian life. I would not have been in Springfield that day if I had gone to D.C. to be with the President at the prayer breakfast.

Following this was a very special event on the horizon. The Billy Graham Association had been conducting what they titled "A Congress on Evangelism" around the world. These events had taken place in other nations. Eventually they scheduled one in the U.S. in Minneapolis. I was selected to be a delegate for our church. Two laymen attended with me. There were possibly 3,000 delegates in attendance.

When we registered, a card was included in the packet that stated a Travel Agency (TLC) would award "one free trip" to the Holy Land. My name was drawn. I could not believe it was for real. When I returned to our church in Springfield and announced what had happened, the congregation immediately decided to send Evelyn with me.

THE GIFT OF A TRIP OVERSEAS

In November of 1969 we flew to New York - then to Rome and on to Greece, and Tel Aviv. It was a 16 day journey that was to impact our lives. The time in Israel was like being on a spiritual journey. Jerusalem, Bethlehem, Hebron, Jericho, the Sea of Galilee, the site of the Sermon on the Mount and the Transfiguration were among the wonderful places we saw.

For several months prior to this trip I was sensing that there would be change in our lives. The confirmation of that happened while we were in Saint Peters Square in Rome. I finally spoke of this to Evelyn while we were standing in the Square. I said to her that we would be stepping into a different world soon, but that we would continue in Christian ministry.

On that same day the Pope was present and spoke from his balcony. He gave his blessing to those present in the Square. We continued our vacation in Rome, visiting Saint Peters Basilica as well as other sites. There were so many historical places to see in this city. The marbled statue of Moses created by Michelangelo is a powerful work of art. When we stepped into Saint Peters Basilica the sound of the Organ came through to us. It was one of the greatest experiences of music a person could have. Also we visited the jail where the Apostle Paul was in chains – the guest of Caesar and the Roman army.

Years later Evelyn and I were at a social event. The conversation moved to a subject that was related to this setting in Rome. Evelyn stated that she was sure that the two of us would make it into the heavenly realm, since we had been converted into the Christian faith earlier and that we had also been blessed by the Pope. This was a stretch that did not go over too well for a rigid fellow who happened to be present.

FROM ROME TO TEL AVIV

Athens was little more than a stop-over. We arrived in Tel Aviv, the major city of Israel for business and commerce. It opened the door to our real destination for this journey. Our travel happened when Ramadan was to be celebrated. This Muslim 'fast' was being observed for 30 days; at least for the day-light hours. In the early hours of each day there was the "Call to Prayer" for the Muslims. A very strange sound in an unknown language, for us, was calling them to pray.

The first day started with a loud blast from an artillery piece. It seemed to shake our hotel room and for sure we thought a war had broken out. No sounds followed so we assumed the peace would hold. Looking out the hotel window we saw a vendor leading a small donkey or burro through the streets. He was selling milk to his customers from a large can on the donkey's back.

The six day war was over, well almost over. On occasion we continued to hear artillery being fired. As travel began for the Tour, we also saw tanks and gunnery destroyed along the roads. Visits were made to cities mentioned before and many more inspirational locations.

To have this experience of visiting the Holy Land was a great time. Each day we were either visiting places where Old Testament events happened or either walking in the footsteps of Jesus or his disciples. Years later I was on Mt. Nebo in Jordan where Moses spent his last days. Later he would appear with Elijah and the Lord on the Mt. of Transfiguration.

As we were nearing the end of our trip the owner of our Tour Bus invited the Group to come to his home for a visit. The meeting was to conclude with all of us sharing Communion. We would be breaking bread and drinking from the Cup in honor of our Lord.

Our group consisted of a variety of people. There were two Roman Catholic Priests; two Episcopalian ladies; three conservative Baptist preachers; two Nazarene Pastors and their wives. A Lutheran pastor was present as well as others. When the Communion time arrived, select people among us drifted away. They had decided they would not be taking Communion with the Group. It was very embarrassing for our Host. It was also embarrassing to the Christian Community. Every leader mentioned above held very important positions in common.

- They all believed in God
- The Trinity was accepted as fact.
- The Holy Bible was looked upon as divinely inspired.
- They believed in love, in mercy and in forgiveness.
- The Savior was important to each of them.
- They believed in His sacrifice. His Resurrection and His Ascension.
- Yet, these Leaders decided they would not take Communion with the group. Remember the man who said... "He

made a circle that left me out. I made a circle that took him in."

Forgive us Father...

It is always good to complete a journey, and return to friends. Since then I have made almost 50 trips overseas to visit the boundless borders of the Christian brotherhood. The Kingdom is much larger than we know.

CHAPTER 7
A NEW BASE

MEETING THE AMERICAN CHURCH

In June of 1971, we had reached the place for decision making. That was a few years ago. Like any change there was risk involved. We needed to understand all of the possibilities that could follow. Things developed slowly, but eventually an actuality opened up for us. Our daughters asked if I intended to move into another profession. I assured them that I would not be moving out of ministry.

Career changes in our world were hard to accept. Threats were made about my decision. One of my fellow pastors asked after I had moved into this new world, "When are you going to return to the ministry?" I shared with him that I had never left. In fact, I was preaching more in this assignment than I was when I was a pastor.

Communication had been established with World Vision International. Through an indirect contact I was able to correspond with Dr. Paul Rees who was Vice President of WV. I had heard him speak on other occasions at select meetings and decided to write him. A request was made for his assistance. He responded very graciously and in a matter of weeks I had an appointment with the midwest Director in their Michigan office. The door opened and I became a representative for them in four states, (Missouri, Kansas, Iowa and Nebraska).

World Vision International is a Christian Relief and Development that serves in many nations of the World. Their work began in Korea serving Orphans while their War was taking place. Since then they serve in select Nations doing multiple task such as Drilling wells, building hospitals, providing medicines, educating children as well as working with Communities in Development programs.

I was to build relationships with churches, colleges, military bases and select companies and individuals. Often we had major events in the larger cities for the purpose of telling the story of WV activities around the world. Usually a gifted singer would provide the program for these events. By word of mouth, endorsements would spread from pastor to pastor that allowed me to speak in many groups. It was an opportunity to build some great relationships with pastors in many denominations.

A new understanding of what really goes on in local churches as it related to leadership came to me in this assignment. Yes, there are some differences found in the many groups of church found in the U.S. One writer suggested that in most cases evangelical churches split hairs over about 2% of that which is important.

Many pastors would be so open with me. Often they felt alone. They did not sense that anyone in their system would listen or understand. If they shared their true feelings they doubted leadership would keep a confidence. This was so painful for them. Across this region I discovered that some of these men would resign if they could do it gracefully. They were 'burnt out' and wanted out.

On a trip to metro St. Louis, I called on a church that was new for us. It was an Assembly of God church. The pastor received me very warmly. We chatted about my purpose for being there and then he mentioned, due to some time restraints, would I come again. He wanted to share with me an experience he had had as he walked through a 40-day fast. The next time I was in St. Louis I went directly to his church. His story was powerful. He began by telling me of a visit to his doctor as he began this journey. He told him of his plans. The doctor was so interested he asked the pastor to please visit with him once a week, at no charge. He wanted to follow his body reactions to such a fast. The doctor asked the pastor to please drink liquids each day.

Then he began to tell me just what happened during this fast.

- The Bible came alive to him like no other time in his life.
- He said his mind was so touched that his preaching was like a fire in his heart. The Holy Scriptures were more powerful as they were shared.
- His opposition was totally confounded by this fresh new leadership.
- He shared with his congregation that certain things that were surfacing in their style of worship was not pleasing to the Lord. Under His leadership, he

called for change that would lift the level of their worship.

He shared this story about what had happened during his fast. One day his secretary called him and let him know that a certain member was being rushed to a hospital. He changed his plans and rushed to the hospital. As he entered the hospital he went by the flower shop and picked up some flowers for this lady. As she was entering the emergency room on a gurney, he placed the flowers in her hands. There had been stress between them. From that day forward she became his friend.

THANKSGIVING DAY SPECIAL

Over the years with World Vision some very special events evolved. It was my privilege to have an appointment with Rev. David Gray, pastor of the Pleasant Green Baptist Church in Kansas City, KS. A very special friendship developed between us. Out of this relationship, Pastor David began to schedule me to come to his church each Thanksgiving Day for four years.

We were living in Springfield, MO at this time. I would arise early on Thanksgiving Day and drive to Kansas City. Traffic was always light on this special day. When I arrived at the church a Thanksgiving celebration would have already begun. The choir was in place. The lady ushers, dressed in beautiful gowns would be caring for those being seated. The music was typical black American style. I loved to be with this congregation. A great turkey dinner was being prepared in the church kitchen. The entire community was invited for this celebration and meal. To preach to a good, lively group like Pastor Gray's was a real joy. The first Thanksgiving an offering was received for the poor of the earth. I remember this gift so well. They gave $2,000 from their hearts. Year after year this great congregation shared with the ministry of World Vision. I rushed home for our Thanksgiving feast each year.

LASTING FRIENDSHIPS

Often in life we know names of groups and possibly a little about what makes them a group. Some special people surfaced in my years with World Vision. The Free Will Baptist churches in Missouri opened their arms to me and invited me into their churches. Lasting friendships were developed with some of these pastors. Dale Skiles and Clarence Burton were key men in this group who opened several doors for World Vision. The Free Will Baptist has over 200 churches in this State.

They also practiced the washing of feet as a part of their worship experience. It appears that most evangelicals pass by this instruction of our Lord. There could be hundreds of reasons they do so. In reality I had never given it much thought until one day Dale Skiles invited me to attend their Annual State Meeting. He simply asked if I would come and wash feet with him. I agreed to participate. When the moment came I wondered what one would experience by practicing this rite my friends believed in. The event unfolded in a very gracious and dignified manner. The ladies present stepped into another room for their foot washing.

After this event my thoughts turned to our Lord who initiated this practice. He did not flow with suggestions that the person needed to be bathed totally, but that the washing of feet would signify the person would experience total humility found in this practice. Maybe His reason for this would be that men's & women's 'feet' were symbolic of that part of the body that was in constant contact with the earth and therefore represent the whole body in its relationship with Life. A current book on the market entitled "The Heavenly Man" written by a Brother Yun tells how the washing of feet brought about a great healing in the House Churches of China.

Another man who was such a friend was Pastor L.D. Souder, a Southern Baptist pastor in Neosho, MO. Our visits were long and rich. Never did we get into a discussion of theology that caused friction. Often he would phone and check with me to see if I had a Sunday evening open and if so, would I please come to his church and preach for him that evening. We were good friends. Military Chaplains were also wonderful in their responses to World Vision.

OVERSEAS WITH WORLD VISION

THE PHILIPPINES, HONG KONG AND TAIWAN

While I was with World Vision I traveled to the Philippines, Hong Kong and Taiwan. This was my third time to visit the Orient. The Navy had already provided two trips. Now I would see the Christian world in action rather than seeing military action. When the Philippine people discovered that I had served in WWII and in the Philippines their level of respect went up.

The first thing to impact me overseas was the existence of poverty like I had never experienced. It was confirmed to me both intellectually and spiritually, that the teaching of Prosperity Christianity is a difficult position to support. The vast majority of Christians throughout the earth live in poverty. Yet, there are thousands of Christians in the west who have been blessed with wealth. A very special responsibility lies upon such people to be good stewards of what they have been blessed with in this world.

However, there is no way that poverty in developing nations will be totally eliminated. We must consider that the 'west' has not been successful to bring change to the North American condition. Strong evidence for this is found in the Appalachians and in any major city ghettos. An effort is being made in today's economy to re-distribute the wealth. After making several trips into the old Soviet Union, China and Eastern Europe one observe the failure of Socialism. Poverty is seldom visible abroad Air Force One, but regardless of who is President or what nation he chooses to visit, poverty will be present.

There is some change in the wind regarding poverty, be it ever so small. Some nations are rising a little in their struggle with poverty.

Fareed Zakaria, in his book *The Post-American World* states that "The share of people living on $1 a day has plummeted from 40% in 1981 to 18 % in 2004 and is estimated to drop to $12 by 2015. Poverty is falling in countries that house 80% of the world's population. There remains real poverty in the world – most worryingly in 50 basket-case countries that contain 1 billion people. China, India and Brazil are the three fastest-growing large economies in the world."

Our Lord confirmed this concept by saying, "The poor will always be with you, somewhere, any place, anytime." Such truths are established by using a world wide measuring stick. The nations who have attempted to practice Socialism or Communism are failing.

BERNIE, THE MAN WHO LIVED UP IN THE AIR

A real lesson in poverty was discovered at Bernie's house in the Philippines. Bernie is a pastor on the island of Palawan in the Philippines. This would be a visit with some folk that we will not forget. Bernie and his wife and their children will hopefully always live in my memory bank. He is a Baptist pastor living at the edge of the world. Poverty lives with Bernie every day.

His house stood on 'stilts' in order to keep high water out when the monsoons came. Living under the house were chickens and monkeys. My friend, Bob Beyer, and I entered their world for an overnight visit. That day Bernie took us to a far away place where life was just outside the Stone Age. It was less than a mile from Bernie's house. We came upon a small group of people living in the jungle. Civilization had not arrived. Women were far behind in the social scheme of things. They were living at a camp site with a common cooking arrangement. A fire was burning for cooking. The clay pots were filled with what they had gathered in the jungle or from the sea. This was no picnic event. We returned to Bernie's home where his wife was cooking a meal for us. She had selected one of her chickens to cook. Never in my life have I ever eaten a chicken that had so little meat on its bones. It appeared this chicken was close to starving to death just before they killed it.

That evening we were taken to an adjoining house where two mattresses were laid out on the floor in two separate rooms. When Bob took off his shoes to retire he noticed that his boots had gotten muddy when he was in the jungle. When we arose the next morning, he discovered his boots had been cleaned.

Someone had slipped into his room and taken his shoes. They were sitting by his mattress, cleaned and ready for the day. Bob came into my room, holding his shoes, crying. He was so touched by this act of kindness. I told Bob it was like having your feet washed by a saint. Possibly Bernie was so far ahead of some of us that we are hardly in the race. Saints sometimes live in poverty.

HOTEL EXTREMES

While on this journey in the southern part of the Philippines we checked into a little hotel for the night. The clerk refused to accept the American Express Travel Checks. I noticed an unusual sign behind the desk. It said, "Please check your guns in for the night." I asked Bob if he would get his gun out so we could conform to the rules of the house. Bob did not have a gun. When we went upstairs to our room and opened the door, bugs and cockroaches went in every direction. We go back to the desk and share our story of the varmints in our room. The desk clerk let us know that he would only refund half of our cost if we chose to leave. We left and went to another facility that was just an inch above the previous hotel. In Manila we stayed at a very clean hotel.

From the Philippines we flew to Hong Kong, the 24-hour city. Landing at the old airport was like slipping into a Star Wars event. The airliner slipped between buildings in a sharp turn, onto the runway, stopping just before you nosed into the Bay. As you flew between the buildings you could almost see the color of the eyes of folk standing at their windows.

A SAINT AND A BUDDIST IN TAIWAN

Out next stop was Taiwan. We would visit some of the Christian Schools that World Vision sponsored. Here we met Sophia, a young married lady who was the Director of World Vision work in this nation. We visited some schools that were under the auspices of the Presbyterian Church. It was interesting to see the culture of these rural people. The schools would entertain us with the children performing their acts. Some of the activities reminded us so much of the Indians who inhabited North America in the earlier day of the U.S.

While in Taiwan we traveled in a van with Sophia as our guide. Sophia was Chinese and in our conversations she shared her deep desire to return to the mainland of China. She and her husband had a small child. Eventually we talked about the risk of returning to China as a Christian. We closed out the day by commenting to her on how costly this could be, even to the loosing of her life. The next morning in the van, Sophia began the day by telling Bob and I that during the night she considered the statement we had made. She immediately stated that she was still committed to returning.

TWO STICKS

Bob and I had some free time one afternoon in Taichung, Taiwan. We went to a Buddhist Temple for a visit. The temple was similar to such a building as you would see in an Oriental movie. As we walked into the area where the high altar was we saw a man standing. The incenses were burning along with candles. We did not intrude, but simply stood and observed. A man was at prayer. He had two wooden sticks in his hands, possibly 14" in length and used these in his moments of prayer. He would stop, stand still, and pitches these sticks in the air about shoulder height. They would fall in this quiet room onto a stone floor. The silence was broken. The sticks bounced and lay in a certain direction. It appeared that he was not satisfied with the results so he picked them up again, waited a moment and pitched them back into the air. Again they fell and this time they seemed to point in the direction that satisfied him. This was the way he approached his Deity in seeking answers to his needs.

How do you address your Deity? Who is your Deity? Every person has a God. In our search for the meaning of life, are we standing in a building that we may call our 'house of God,' pitching our sticks into the air, hoping for a magical answer. There is no magic to be found in a place where the Cross is standing; where the hope of a Resurrection is extended. Regardless of the rejections to the Deity of our Lord in this culture, He is the same – yesterday, today and forever. He will not crumble when some unbelievable storm attempts to wash everything away from you. He is trustworthy.

CAMBODIA

Later in December of 1994, it was my privilege to visit Cambodia. Buddha was King in this ancient land and violence was a way of life. Poverty and evil have been present a long time. The world will never forget Pol Pot, a leader who murdered over 3,000,000 people, most of whom were the educated of the nation.

We made a thee-hour boat ride to visit Anghor Wat. A huge temple was built near the City of Siem Reap. This mass of ruins extends for an approximate mile. Built in the 12th century, it had been a marvelous temple complex where false gods were worshipped. We stopped in the ruins and had a worship time with our God, the Creator of the Universe.

Angkor Wat paled in our eyes compared to what was about to happen. Earlier I shared with you that I do not make a good tourist. Anghor Wat was for tourists. It is a great place to see from an historical view.

A HOSPITAL VISIT – A SAINT -- A VISIT WITH A DICTATOR

Years earlier, while I was on the staff of World Vision in the U.S., it was my privilege to present to groups the opportunity of building a Children's Hospital in Cambodia. While in Cambodia on this trip I asked that I be taken to see this Hospital. When we arrived and saw this beautiful, but simple building. I was on cloud nine. Little children were in wards that were related to their need. The medical care was superb. No where had I ever seen such a nice facility designed to serve the health needs of children in the developing nations.

As we walked through these grounds we came upon a van. Painted on the door of the van were these words: "Donated by Kanakuk Kamps, Joe White, Director." When I served with World Vision I had met Joe at one of the several summer camps he and his father had developed. During the summer, youth would come for training. These young people were from upper middle class homes as well as from the ghettos of Denver, Dallas, Kansas City and Houston. They were located south of Branson, MO. This camping program is one of the most outstanding Christian summer camping programs for youth in the U.S.

During my years with World Vision Joe and I became friends. Joe was interested and became involved with World Vision. He allowed me to speak at one of these camps. It was an honor. I am so grateful to this man for his involvement with World Vision. Little did I ever realize someday I would be in Cambodia and see the fruit of his gift and of the privilege I had in challenging him to become involved with this project as well as others.

After returning from Cambodia I went to see Joe White. I told him of my experience of seeing the van he had given and that I had a photo of the van for him. I attempted to give Joe the photo and he quickly stated, "No, please, I do not need to see this photo." I have never forgotten his response. He simply did not want any praise for his gift.

So often, life seems to match us up with some task that has a deeper purpose within it that we do not recognize. It is something that will help us to rise to another level, only if we will walk humbly, not looking for accolades.

THE SAINT

Meeting Barnabas, a young Cambodian man who had converted to Christianity in the land of Buddha, was one of the highlights of my travels. Barnabas was born to a respected Buddhist family. His father had been a monk, but had laid aside his robe to marry.

At eighteen Barnabas worked for the Communist party. He was assigned to check out the activities happening in the churches of Cambodia. He found no connection of illegal activity. One night his work led him to attend a crusade conducted by Stan Mooneyhan of World Vision. The spirit of the Lord touched him and Barnabas was converted. His father and mother turned against him. They refused to feed him on Sundays when he returned home after attending church.

His family sent him to a Pogada, a place for Buddhist teaching and training. He remained true to his faith. The family thought he had become a Catholic. He studied his Bible. When he came to Exodus 20 where the Ten Commandments were recorded, he accepted the teaching that he was to honor his father and mother. He told them about this teaching. At this time they begin to rethink how they had treated him. A strain had developed in the past between him and his sister. The parents asked him, "Will you recognize and forgive your sister." He said, "Yes." It was then that his father's heart softened toward him.

After spying on World Vision they offered him a job. His parents needed support and he provided it. They told others of their son's support. "Our son is honoring us while we live, not after our death."

PRISON TIME FOR THE SAINT

Later he returned to his home and found it empty. The Khmer Rouge had come and destroyed so much. He never found his parents later in life. He was arrested near Viet Nam and put in prison. The brain washing began. His possessions included one pair of pants and a shirt. It was the darkest hour of his life. They had taken his Bible and pencil.

While other prisoners slept, he would pray. He spoke Psalms 23 over and over as he lived in the shadow of death. Songs he had heard in church came to him. He remembered *How Great Thou Art*. He was the last to sleep and the first to rise. Working in the rice paddies, he would rejoice when he heard the rain falling because he could then shout out his prayers and songs. It was the best of times to sing when the rain was falling hard.

While offering prayer over his meal other prisoners would steal his food. The guards asked him why he would pray. It would open the door for him to share his story of his life in Christ. The guards discussed this and brought charges against Him. You are involved with an American Organization. You are an imperialist dog. You are the son of noble birth. You are a Christian. Their verdict was decided. "Because you work hard and rise early, we will let you live. Yet, you are a big suspect." They made him do odd jobs – like serving as an ox pulling a cart. Barnabas said, "I cannot complain, it is the school of humility that I learned in church." The guards were amazed.

His health remained good. They allowed him to bath in a nearby stream.

One day the guards announced that he was to become the camp cook. As a son of a privileged family he had never worked in the rice paddies or fished the rivers. He now was a prisoner among prisoners. All of these prisoners were from the upper level of Cambodian society – teachers, government officials, doctors and nurses.

One of Barnabas' duties was to serve fish on a given day of the week. He was to catch the fish for these meals. He rose at 4 am while the moon was still shining. He went to a paddy that had been drained. As he stood in this dry paddy he began to pray. From adjoining paddies, fish began to jump from the flooded fields into the dry field. He gathered up his catch and served the fish for lunch.

Months passed and his health began to fail. He became so weak he was unable to return to the barracks. A guard saw him. Barnabas told him he was dying. "Please take me to the camp authorities. I have done my best." When the guard reported this to his authorities one of them ordered that he be brought to the officers quarters. They prepared a great meal for Barnabas and gave him extra salt.

Eight of these prisoners survived this ordeal. One is a secretary of state in the present government. Two others became leaders in the nation. Barnabas sees these men on occasion as he travels the country to preach.

Barnabas, at the conclusion of our interview said, "We have no reason to doubt God's wisdom. Every major need of our lives He will give help and direction. After listening to this man for two hours I believed that I had seen and heard a man who proved that by grace a person can live out the *Sermon on the Mount*. You can find a copy of this written by Matthew in the Great Book, The Bible.

POL POT, THE DICTATOR

I Met Pol Pot in Cambodia. This vicious dictator and murdered is gone, but his presence is evident everywhere. We visited his "killing fields." We saw sites that were established for the sole purpose of exhibiting the *skulls* of those he had ordered to be killed.

There is actually a field where an A frame building is standing. The entire end of the building is open to the public that can be viewed. A glass wall stands with shelf after shelf of the skulls of the people he killed. Behind this building there is a *killing field* with multiple graves.

Only a few men in the world have become so evil until the knowledge of their existence can only be defined by ONE word ---- "EVIL"

AFTER RETIREMENT

After retirement a new venue opened up. A new format was needed in order to carry on a reputable and legitimate response to the many needy areas that had surfaced from the wealth of experience that had come to us. There are no words that can express the satisfaction of what was to be discovered as these opportunities opened.

GLOBAL EDUCATION PLUS, INC., was created. It is a 501© non-profit corporation. The GEP vision surfaced and has expanded over 16 years. It has served in select nations such as China, Romania, Russia and the Ukraine as well as Latin America. Pastor training events were scheduled. GEP later expanded by becoming involved with Private Christian Schools. There are hundreds of these schools functioning overseas. We have provided textbooks, classroom equipment, vitamins, as well as copiers, etc. Scholarships are shared to upgrade select teachers as well as the underwriting of Extension education training events for teachers in these schools. Over the last three years, five of these Events have been completed. Five new school houses have been built along with remodeling of several existing buildings. GEP is also involved with a children's education program in China.

After my World Vision days I attempted to retire. Don't do it! If you have good health, a good mind, as well as some 'fire in your belly', find something to do. It was never meant for a husband to hang around the house, punishing his wife, getting in the way. Do something my friend. Ladies have found ways and means of continuing to contribute and be a force for great causes after retirement.

You should not quit. Pray, and ask the Lord to help you find something to do. Make the change with dignity. If you are a carpenter, or a plumber, or an electrician, do repair jobs for widows. I know a PhD who does 'School crossing guard' work. He takes his earnings and goes to China once a year to serve in extension education for Chinese teachers.

I have a friend named Jake Beadle who is such a man. For years after he retired as an employee of the Frisco Railroads, he blessed people by the hundreds just doing little jobs.

He bought a van and filled it with his tools. At his church there were several widow ladies. Off he went to work, doing everything under the sun. He also assisted in a downtown mission with their repair work.

At the time I was so blessed to be traveling the world, doing ministry work with pastors and school children. Jake kept our home functioning with his carpenter work, his plumbing and electrical skills. He would always say to me, "You do your work and I will keep you free of such things that I can do." He really was a part of our lives at that time. Since I am a person with no mechanical skills, I was really glad to have such a friend.

Most of our life has been defined by simply asking the question, "What do you do for a living?" The usual answer is something like an accountant, or executive or pipefitter or school teacher. When you retire the only word for some is "I am retired." Let me suggest you might come to grips with another answer. Why not say, if you have found something to do at this stage, "I am an Entrepreneur." In fact, at 50, against all odds, I was confident that I should move on to another field. Some of my friends thought I had lost my bearings, while others really wished they could join me.

For awhile, things were slow to open, but the years have proven otherwise.

We live in a culture that has taken away a lot of the challenge. We really do rely on government, institutions, corporations, churches, welfare, and entitlements. Do we say "They own something to me?" 'We have given our lives to this job." This thinking will not stand. Writing this in the year of the Lord, 2009, many are coming to understand more clearly that life could become hard in the West, Like 10,000,000 unemployed or more. We have are already discovering that the 'world is flat,' with many of the jobs going overseas.

CHAPTER 8
ENTREPRENEUR DAYS

EASTERN EUROPE AND THE OLD SOVIET UNION

A friend of mine, Dr. Jim Mugg, was pastor of a strong church in Springfield, Missouri, decided to make a change. He had already established a 'pastor training' program in Romania and later invited me to travel to Romania with him. Romania at that time was going through an upheaval. Like all of Eastern Europe, Communism had become entrenched in this land. President Ceausescu was a dictator. No one ever expected him to fall. At the close of his reign he was still defiant. A week before he was executed by a firing squad he ordered the killing of demonstrators in Timisoara, one of the most beautiful cities in the country. Bucharest residences knew the fury of his hate. The Securitate (KGB) were present everywhere. Visiting in this nation was dangerous. Jim had been escorted out of the nation once, but he continued to return and meet with the pastors.

President Iliescu came into power, but he represented the same political system. One Romanian told me that 'we have traded one dictator for another.' On this, my first trip into this nation, I sensed the oppression at the Bucharest Airport. The hassle began with cab drivers. Jim and I spent a few days in the capitol before we ventured into the interior.

One night we left our simple little hotel and went to the International Hotel for dinner. It was located in the heart of Bucharest. Outside the hotel we walked through groups of students demonstrating against the government. Tanks were standing by. As we entered the hotel the environment changed. It was a beautiful lobby. The major dining room was as nice as most large hotels in the U.S. A lovely lady, dressed in an evening gown, was playing classical music on a white grand piano. The meal was great. What a contrast to what was going on in the street. It was late and dark just beyond the door of this beautiful hotel. The streets were full of angry, oppressed people. When we returned to our hotel, we were not at ease in our rooms.

The next morning we boarded a train for Timisoara where our first meeting with a group of a dozen pastors was to be conducted. At our first stop, three young soldiers boarded the train. Each of them had an AK-47 strapped over their shoulders. I doubt if any of the three was 20 years old. As we looked into their young faces we hoped they would not challenge us. Considering what we had witnessed the night before in Bucharest we had concerns.

We visited seven churches on this trip. The pastors would gather in an apartment for a meal, followed by Jim teaching these men in a prescribed course on each trip. The shades would be shut very tight with the session lasting 2 hours or so. All of these men lived literally under the gun of Communism. We traveled from Bucharest, to Timisoara and then on to Oradea. Next was the church in Zalau and Bisterita.

Our final stop was on the east coast of the Black Sea. Here we met with a physicist, Octavian Baban. He hoped to schedule a training program in Constanta. The day was hot and in the evening while we slept the Mosquitoes visited us in mass. We slept on one of the worst beds in the whole universe. As a boy I began with Mosquitoes in Texas off the salt grass prairies. Later I linked up with them again in New Guinea for a Malaria bout. Here I am now on the Black Sea at another Mosquitoes party.

Daniel Cocar was the pastor of the Third Baptist Church in Timisoara. When Billy Graham was in Romania he spoke in this church. Paul Negrut, was a Psychologist and a former pastor of Second Baptist church in Oradea. He had hopes of going to England to work on his PhD. Nicole Manzat was pastor of the Baptist Church is Bistria. This church had a huge building that seated 800. The Communists had fought his progress and eventually bull-dozed this church to the ground in 1982. It took them four years to rebuild. Bistria was a beautiful city.

THE CHURCH AT ITS BEST

On the upcoming Sunday, Nicolae decided to take us to another city, Topolovat, for services. His associate remained in Bistria and preached for him. When we arrived at this small church just outside the city we were glad. It was located on a beautiful hillside. The day was beautiful. First we were to have a worship service, then march about half a mile to a nice flowing river for a baptismal event.

The church service was different. They had a six member orchestra playing the hymns. It was all brass except for one Clarinet. These instruments would have never been purchased in a garage sale in the U.S. The Church seated about 50 people. There must have been 90 in the room. Speaker after speaker addressed the congregation with praise and thanksgiving. This was their first baptismal service since the ironfisted Nicolae Ceausescu's reign began 24 years ago.

Eventually they asked Jim and me to speak. The day, so hot inside, the Chapel so packed with people; I choose to simply greet them. To share of our common Christian faith and let them know what an honor it was for us to just be in their presence. We were very close in this small building. I could see deeply into their faces and see what the years of oppression had done to them. It was an experience where the love of God made us one. Tears came to my eyes. Tears came to their eyes. They did not have beautiful, clean, laundered handkerchiefs to wipe away the tears; just a simple piece of old cloth. It was so good to be with God's people that day.

THE LORD HAS CHILDREN ALL OVER THE EARTH

These children are to be found on every continent. Their hands are calloused from hard labor, both women and men. They exist in and under every kind of governmental system that can be found. They till the soil. Some are sentenced to prison for His Name's sake. Some have a very hard Life. These 21st Century Christians realize that the Apostle Paul of the 1st Century also spent much time in prison. So this was nothing new as they reflected on Paul's life.

TWO BAPTISMAL EVENTS JOINED – WATER AND FIRE

When we finished our worship service we began to gather in front of their church. Plans had been made to march to the river. The band was out front. They were playing *Onward Christian Soldiers.* Down the hill we walked singing the song as the band struggled to pull the music together. The band was not the greatest, but they had their heart in it. This cohesive group of Christians was making a statement to their city. Moving onto the main street of Topolovat we advanced to the river. I am not sure how many were baptized; possibly two dozen. It was one great day for the Faith. The town people were on the street to see this rare event. They followed to the river bank to watch this Christian act of Baptism. Communism took a back seat. When we arrived at the riverside, all of the preachers had to wax elegantly. It was hot and sometimes Preachers don't know when to quit. As each person went into the water they carried a beautiful rose. As they were baptized they cast their rose on the flowing stream of a clean river. What a day! A real, in your face event, that states the Christian Faith does survive in its encounter in evil situations. Another baptism In Romania took place in a very muddy river.

Many of this group had their own fiery torment from the hand of the Communist. Some had experienced jail and harassment from the Securitate (Secret Police). At one of the pastor's training sessions Jim Mugg, the teacher, asked if any of them had ever had a time in their lives when they sensed they were lifted to a higher plane or another level in their Christian life; something beyond their conversion in the Christian faith. A pastor immediately responded and began to tell of the time when he knew he was stepping up to another level in his faith.

"One morning the Securitate showed up at the door of our home. They stormed in and began ransacking the house. Their main interest was my library. They began to empty desk drawers, pulling books out of their shelves. They were looking for anti-government publications. As I stood in the hallway of my house, a new strength entered my life. There was a 'presence' beyond anything I had ever known that became a new reality in my faith. It was a peace that overcame my enemies. They were the slaves. I was the free man."

CROSSING THE BORDER

`Other trips were made into Romania. A church leader by the name of Jonel was the pastor in Isai, Romania. This city was located in the north east corner of the country. It was near the border of Moldova. Two scheduled Pastor Conferences were presented here. Later, a group of University students from the U.S. traveled with us to this city along with a trip into Moldova, one of the nations of the old Soviet Union. Crossing the border into Moldova was a time consuming event. Often, going through these passport inspections as well as having to experience the risk of some fluke thing regarding luggage, was such a waste of time. But these Bureaucrats, who man Custom Offices at entrance points in most developing nations, act in unimaginative ways, insisting on procedures being followed, initiative given them out of their small power base.

In Moldova we also visited a school as well as a 'Refugee Camp'. The team of college students quickly adjusted to this packed environment of children along with their mothers. For possibly two to three hours it was like a picnic atmosphere. Games took place without equipment. Laughter and loving these children was just what was needed for the moment. The children followed us to our Van, clinging to American students. Some of the children were crying, not wanting to see our Van leave.

Returning to Romania in our two Vans we experienced an accident. One of the Vans was being driven by Colin Boyland, a co-traveler who resided in London. Standing on the side of a highway, just after our passing though customs, a small child unexpectedly rushed out in front of our Van. The driver quickly responded turning into a low level area alongside the road. The child was caught in this path, but was not injured. She was in the low part of the ditch as the Van passed over her. The authorities came and the hassle began.

They eventually allowed us to enter the city of Isai, but required that we spend an extra day to make sure the child was not injured in any way. Our friend from London was released. We were so thankful to God that our Driver and the group were not detained for a hearing and a court trial.

ST. PETERSBURG, RUSSIA

In late March of '99, I traveled alone to St. Petersburg, Russia. From there the next stop was Kiev, Ukraine. In St. Petersburg, a Primary/Secondary school teachers training event was scheduled. 250 teachers were present. There were five representatives from the Association of Christian Schools present. Each had come to share and train these leaders.

The city itself, after seven decades of Communism, was in need of great repair. The streets were still covered with some snow. Little if any repairs had been made for years it appeared. Street lights were inadequate. The buildings had been so neglected that they were hardly inhabitable. Yet life moved on. The people, in most instances, were poorly dressed. To have a job was a sign of success. The famous circus of St. Petersburg was still functioning. It was indeed a welcomed Event to attend. To have any kind of entertainment available for these people was a surprise.

The conference went well. There were teachers present from Christian Schools as well as State schools. In fact, the State schools were thrilled to attend such an event. Nothing of any significance was provided for them by the State. Our purpose for being there was to critique what ACSI was doing for the schools. The President of ACSI, Dr. Ken Smitherman and his wife were present. Attending this Conference was helpful by giving us direction as to how we could support these schools.

At the airport in St. Petersburg an interesting thing developed. Anyone that travels internationally should be ready at all times for surprises. Custom people, as has been mentioned, can be very difficult as well as very sharp. You do not insult them. It is their country and you are a guest. You keep your mouth closed and your ears and eyes open. If you press a point, you may be looking at a jail cell, or you may have to bribe your way out of Town. Bribes are common. On this scheduled flight a very unwise response developed from a Traveler who could have found himself in jail. The Custom official was very generous by not allow the event to become a serious incident.

I LOVE KIEV

There is an amazing Boulevard that exists in Kiev. Some very exclusive shops are located here along with a very nice department store. A good restaurant is located in this store. To walk this street was a pleasure. An excellent statue of Lenin still stands here. For some time McDonalds has had one of their fast food restaurants in Kiev. Naturally, we chose to have lunch at McDonalds in Kiev. Earlier we had been in McDonalds in Moscow.

On one of our trips to Kiev it appeared the flu was coming my way. I simply walked into a Drug Store and purchased the same medicine my U.S. doctor prescribed for me, without a prescription. In Kiev this Medicine cost $ 3 plus. Twice we were able to go to a Opera House in Kiev. The 'White Swan' was scheduled one evening. Like Moscow, Kiev has a wonderful subway system. We always had local Christians to manage our travel. They assisted us in the cities, the Country and at Airports. They constantly keep watch over us, especially the food we ordered in restaurants. Their Cars and Vans were old and rough. Seldom would any vehicle have shock absorbers. Riding in such a car was like riding on a mule without a saddle; something I have never done.

Sometimes accountability requirements were not always present. A school could be on the verge of collapse due to debt or it could be weak in its leadership team. Our policy was to observe and critic a school. Then we would decide on our involvement or non-involvement. It was never in our mind to bail schools out that were lacking in their management skills or deep in debt. Over a 15-year period we had to wisely walk away from some things that had the marks of failure plain and visible. In a 15 year span, we encounter only four or five situations.

Kiev had several Christian Schools. Usually they would have been created under the leadership of a strong lady with a Christian worldview. Very few men were Principals. These educators would always tell us that the PhD's earned in their world were much better than any degree you would earn in the West. I never argued with them regarding this view since all I have is a lowly B.S.

Their schools were to be found in old deserted buildings, old factories that had been deserted, or in a high rise apartment house where they would have rented a floor. We did work with only one school that actually had a real school house. The services we provided in the old Soviet Union were textbooks, a few Computers, classroom equipment, some play ground items and other small things. The ACSI people would ask us where and how Global Education Plus came up with such a plan. It was a gift to us from our Lord.

While we were in Kiev I was invited to speak at a University. A friend of mine from America was living in Kiev and had a contract with this school. I was a classmate of his father's in college. One of Dr. John Johnson classes was for students majoring in Sociology. Dr. Johnson explained to me that all of his students in this class spoke and wrote English. They were exceptional students. He asked that I give a brief overview of what life was like for me during the seven decades I had lived in America. It was a great time to share with them as they questioned me at the end of the class. When I shared about being a minister, it was very difficult for them to comprehend. It appeared they had never had any relationships with an Orthodox Priest.

Over the years in the old Soviet Union, the western social structure would show up. How they loved the movies out of Hollywood. Some really came to believe that everything in our movies was how it really is in America. One day I discovered that the most famous of all our television shows was "Dallas". To tell them that possibly 1% of America lived at this level of wealth was a disappointment to them.

TATIANA, THE GIANT KILLER

Several trips were made into the Ukraine. On one occasion we went to the far east side of the State. The bus ride was eight hours one way. The city was named Kharkov. Three Christian schools were located there. The city also had one of the nicest Opera Houses that had been built years ago. To spend an evening here was a delight. Before we arrived in Kharkov an arrangement had been made for a very special lady to meet us. She was a Principal of a School. She was coming by train from across the border in Russia. Her name was Tatiana. I can actually visualize her standing in my presence even now.

We discovered quickly that this lady was really engaged with life. Her days were extremely difficult as a widow. Her husband was an Officer in the Russian Military. He was a helicopter pilot in their Air Force. The military had sent him to Afghanistan. He had been shot down and died from his injuries.

Tatiana weighed heavily the possibilities of going to the U.S. as a refugee with her children. She investigated the opportunity, but decided against the plan. She was a Christian as well as an educator. She decided to remain in Russia and open a Christian Primary School. She would invest her talents and energies in Russia.

She discovered this would not be an easy task. Yes, there had been changes with Mr. Mikhail Gorbachev. New thinking for the country and the world was taking place. Gorbachev had written that "We are all passengers aboard one ship, the earth, and we must not allow it to be wrecked. There will be no second Noah's Ark." I was amazed that he would mention Noah. He did not understand that there is a rescue effort in place when all the earth will bow before a supreme Deity.

Even with Perestroika being introduced to the nation, not every one was buying into the program. On a previous trip to the Ukraine our Team was teaching a group of pastors a lesson on forgiveness. There were 25 present in the classroom. This was in the city of Korsten, Ukraine, located 90 miles north of Kiev. In fact, it was a short distance from Chernobyl where the nuclear power plant exploded. One day in this meeting one of the pastors did exploded. He said he would never forgive Gorbachev for introducing Perestroika to Russia. That was an interesting moment with no resolution. This unusual comment was strange when we realized a Christian Pastor was in agreement with the leader of the Communist Party.

These local authorities that Tatiana was asking to give accreditation to her school continued to function as communist in the Stalin mind set. They were not about to surrender their power base. They were too far removed from Moscow. They had turf to protect. At every turn, the locals in power were resisting Tatiana in the establishing of a Christian school.

Tatiana would arrange for these meetings with this regional group. She continued to pursue her goals for the school she had started. Every time they would listen but refuse to grant her this status. Finally one day, as she was in another meeting with them, she stopped the proceeding, placed her huge purse on the table and said, "I need to make a phone call to my teachers and students. I will ask them to begin praying that our accreditation will be approved." She made her call and returned to the Conference Room. She took her seat, placed the documents in front of the Chairman and declared to him, ""It is time to sign these forms declaring that our school is a registered, legal school in Russia." The chairman became as meek as a little lamb, picked up his pen and signed the documents.

Before Tatiana left the room, the chairman asked her to pray for his son who was seriously ill. She promised she would. Tatiana had engaged those forces that will always challenge. This kind of opposition will try to keep one from raising their voice. Obstacles and opponents will do any and everything possible to keep one from engaging in their purpose of life. These events did not happen overnight. Tatiana went through time and space for her own development as a believer. Vision comes as people sense human need and respond. Little by little things evolve and surface, maturing, in order that plans can be formalized in the mind and the heart. Eventually response and change can happen, if we don't give up.

There is a photo of this lady made in Kharkov where we met. As she departed to return to her school in Russia, She lifted her arm and fist into the air, confirming that she planned to be faithful. Our Agency placed $1,000 in her hands for the school. It was one of the best gifts ever given by Global Education Plus.

Tatiana sensed the need for the school. She responded through her faith that was at work in her life. She applied her talent, her training and her passion. She did it through the pain of losing her husband to death. She chose to stay in Russia, doing a task that challenged her best efforts. She formalized her vision by being creative, opening a school. She found her voice and used it.

When a person finds their voice it will expand their influence. Not for the purpose of maneuvering, or manipulating, or controlling people, but rather to inspire them. All of us need to break free of our own selfish interest, thinking of the other person's need. That would call for one to break with 'old ways' and 'old thinking' as it relates to self interest.

There is this matter of grace that could be discovered. It is not a cheap means to a selfish end, but rather it's a Presence that will cause you to grow from the inside out. You will be willing to pray and think. For sure, one will no longer look on people as pawns to be used, but see them for their true worth. In recent years I have been in dozens and dozens of children's classrooms around the world. It is staggering to imagine the potential that is present among them. There is a phrase in the Sermon on the Mount that says "Keep on Asking…

Keep on Seeking…Keep on Knocking." (Amplified translation)

CLASSROOMS ARE IMPORTANT

A classroom can have an amazing variety of personalities present - possibly a Samuel, a David, Timothy, even a Demas or a Judas. Maybe Ruth and Esther, Lois and Rachel, maybe even a Jezebel. It may be that you might not know some of these persons who once were kids. Their stories are in the Book. Who will succeed? Who will be mediocre, who will fail? Every school needs a Tatiana present who will engage the world; teaching the basics along with a Value System that gives direction to a life with a Christian Worldview.

A DIFFERENT KIND OF COMMUNION

Remember the Communion service that fell apart in Jerusalem? The one that got all mixed up over strange lines that had been drawn in the sand? Where divisions and turf protection along with bias and divisions had taken up residents in the souls of good people? Well, before I left Kharkov one time, a friend took me to an old theatre that had been abandoned. The auditorium was a disaster. The seats were broken and worn out. A church was meeting in this building. They invited us to share greetings with the body. At the close of the service they were serving Communion. Possibly half of the people appeared to be sick with a cold, or the influenza. It was winter. The group used the common cup passing it from one to another. I considered whether to participate only because I did not want to get sick in their world. We did not give a single thought that we would refuse the Cup because of whom they were or who we were. The Cup appeared. I prayer and took the wine. Yes, it was wine! God is good.

STREET SERVICES – NIGHT BAPTIZING

Previously we mentioned that in Korsten, we had a pastor's class with 25 men. The men we discovered here were amazing. Pastor Kaminchi was the senior man among them. He looked so much like Mark Twain. Many years prior to this time He had been arrested and sentenced to 25 years in a Gulag Camp in Siberia. He was released after 5 years in this Gulag. In this same Gulag Camp there was a young lady from Korsten, his home town. Upon their release they returned to their home city and were married.

Before going to prison Pastor Kaminchi had developed some very unique methods of keeping his congregation bonded together. They were denied the privilege of having worship in their church building. He organized some ways of overcoming the Communist control. First, Ten or so of these Believers would meet on the sidewalks of Korsten and casually have a worship service. It would be a market day. They would stand and appear to just be talking to one another. All the time prayers were being made. Scripture was being quoted. Conversational preaching was happening. Everyone would keep their eyes open, continually observing people nearby. Multiple events like this would take place on Saturdays. In the earlier days of our Country, people of rural towns and communities would come to town on Saturday to do their business. So it was in Korsten, only these Russians would be in worship while the markets were busy.

The Congregation would also plan their baptism services at Night. It would be a late hour when others of the Community would be asleep. These Christians would quietly move out to the riverside in preparation for this baptism. Guards would be posted to warn the people if some of the authorities would discover their meeting place. Being arrested was a possibility.

The Courage to take a Risk had consequences.

Pastor Kaminchi had spent five years in the Gulag. Stalin is gone. Some way or another, such men will always disappear. Now this Pastor has a strong congregation that he serves. They can now worship in their own building. There is a beautiful scripted verse on the wall above the baptismal Font in this church.

"Come unto me and I will give you rest."

FATHER AND SON

At the western edge of the Ukraine there is a city named Chernovtsy. It borders Romania and Moldova. The population is approximately 242,000. The city is extremely old and very typical in style of this region. The Prut River runs through this area and is a tributary of the Danube. It was located west of Kiev, the capitol. Twice we went by train to Chernovtsy – an all night journey. Two trips were made in a worn out van.

I became acquainted with the Kushnir family by meeting their daughter Vera in the U.S. We met her at a church service where she sang.

Her English was very good. She also was an outstanding soloist. An invitation was given by Vera to bring a Team to visit their Christian School as well as their Church.

Over the years four trips were made to this city. Juriy, was a brother of Vera who served as a regional overseer of several Baptist Churches in the area. He had a wonderful family and several children. One of his children was a boy named Max. He had studied English and was an excellent interpreter for us. Max was about twelve years old. He was also one of the best Interpreters we had worked with anywhere in the world. Juriy and Max were bonded as father and son. All of the Team loved this family.

It was my privilege to also visit Juriy's father and mother in their little home. Vera, the daughter, took me to their home. Pastor Kushnir had served a church in Chernovtsy for many years while the Communists were in power. He and his wife represented the finest of the finest of this world. All over the world I kept meeting people that I knew would be at the head of the line some day. You know – 'the last shall be first.'

During our visit to their home we had a meal. It consisted of potatoes, tomatoes, cucumbers and hard bread. Near their house one could see a little garden plot. After our meal, Pastor Kushnir began to share his story with me. His daughter Vera was setting in the room. I was about to hear another great account of one who had experienced the real test of life as it relates to Christian Faith. The Communist arrested this pastor. They began asking questions, wanting to know who the people were that met under cover of darkness to worship. Later he was charged and convicted. He was sentences to prison in his home town of Chernovtsy.

This prison had devised a way to make a person talk. They had built a metal cage with sharp pointed arrows welded to the frame, pointing inward. It was also designed so that two sides of the cage could be moved into the body of the person in the cage. A cranking devise would be turned, moving the two sides into the prisoner's body. They would demand that the pastor give the names of his flock. He refused to confess. Finally, they would back off on the crank handle. After several attempts, they gave up and released him. When he finished sharing the story of his imprisonment his daughter Vera turned to me and said, "This is the first time I have ever heard my father tell this." She was crying.

Vera was a small child when this happened. Later, Pastor Kushnir and I, along with my friend Ron Dickson, were standing on a street corner in Chernovtsy, looking at a large yellow building. It was the prison where he had been incarcerated for being a faithful pastor.

In Chernovtsy our group conducted two pastor training events. Our guest teachers on this trip were Gerald Diddle, a retired CEO with a large electrical power distribution system, and Charles Baldwin, a retired professor who was a scholar in Greek and Hebrew along with David Schooler, a pastor residing in Ohio. Ron Dickson was a retired TWA airline pilot.

In one of our closing events we had a question and answer time with these sixty pastors. One of these men stood and asked, "How do American Pastors understand and practice the holy kiss that the Apostle Paul wrote about?" Well, we fumbled with what to say. Finally we said that it was not the custom of men believers in the West to use this in our greeting of one another.

After the session adjourned, the Pastor who had asked the question started down the aisle of the church headed for me. When he arrived he put a 'big Russian bear hug' on me. Next, he started for the 'holy kiss.' I was able to escape without injury.

We gave gifts to the pastor and the school each time we visited. On one occasion, as we were preparing to leave for the day, the Principal of the school asked us to please buy them a large hot water heater for their school. These water heaters were available in Chernovtsy. The school had a water delivery system in the building. We agreed and gave them the money. Before we left that day, the heater had been installed.

THE CARPENTER PREACHER

Aeroflot, the Russian Airline, at that time was not safe. Flying from Moscow to Odessa our only choice was Aeroflot. These planes were really dangerous. The interior of this plane was so worn out you could hardly find a seat that did not need repairs. Yet the plane was full. With the interior in shambles, it made one wonder about the jet engines. On arriving in Odessa our bags were lost. It was three nights before our luggage showed up. No one had called us to tell of the luggage arrival. Taking a chance of their arrival the Three of us went to the airport from our hotel and found our luggage setting outside in the rain. There was no one on duty.

Odessa sets on the shoreline of the Black Sea. This will be my third time to look across this body of water. In former days Odessa was a major port for the old Soviet Union's Navy as well as a commercial port. Old is hardly a word that describes the Soviet Union.

Our reason for visiting Odessa was the existence of three Christian Schools that were under the umbrella of the Association of Christian Schools International. Their continued existence was always perilous due to the lack of funding and facilities. It was always interesting to see them making do with very little.

We met Victor, the carpenter preacher, in Odessa. He is a classic example of survival in this bleak and desolate world. He did not have a choice in the place where he had been planted. If I understood him and his thinking, he probably never struggled with the word 'successes from a secular worldview of life. At the time we met he was serving a church in Odessa. Prior to this time he was a traveling minister. He had a family and worked as a carpenter. He also owned an old car.

In the Ukraine he would pack his family into their car and move to a small city. He had just left a former 'house church' where he had been under surveillance. In each city he would gather a small group for worship. The KGB would be on his trail. When this gathering of Christians would surface, he would move his family to another city. He did odd jobs to sustain his family.

Later in life I wondered just what it means to succeed. Who really knows the true definition of success? In small towns and large cities, you will find some very different people who have come to their own understanding of what success is. Did I read something one time that went like this? "A person's life is not to be measured by what he has accumulated." For sure there is a host of ideas, as well as people who seem to have all of the answers as how we are to measure success. In my younger days, just after finishing the University, an associate in the business I was involved in shared with me that he did not think I would succeed. His decision was made on the question of my not being involved in cocktail hour at business meetings. To this day I remember saying to this co-worker. "Really, I do not have to succeed." For sure, by the measuring stick he had used on me, I would not succeed. Be sure you have the right measuring stick when you are searching for the meaning of life.

I have a sense that VICTOR could well be at the head of the line.

A VISIT AT THE ODESSA AIRPORT

Three of us had just left Victor and were on our way to the Odessa Airport. After checking in we had a long wait for our flight. Since we thought the only English speaking people present was our group, we had a very open conversation going. Soon a gentleman came over and introduced himself in English. After hearing so much conversation in the native tongue one is always glad to make contact with your language group. The Gentleman asks us why we were in the Ukraine. He also shared that he had taught at the University of Texas. We told him our story of why we were in the Ukraine with an emphasis as it related to our faith.

He was very open and receptive. He began to share his understanding of the Soviet System. After some talk he said, "if we Russians had not taken the road of resistance to the Christian faith, that it well could have been different and better." I then responded by saying to him, "Possibly it is not too late. It would take men like you, well educated as well as dedicated Christians to turn your culture in a better direction." His response was deafening. He looked at me carefully in the eyes, and never said a word. He slowly returned to be with his group. Even as I write these words I pray for him.

Our flight back to Kiev was again on an Aeroflot plane. It was another plane that was worn out on the inside. There were two traveling companions who were seated ahead of me. My seat was in the midst of a group of Ukrainians who enjoyed their flight listening to me 'snore' my way through the night. Sleeping on such trips was an achievement.

A CONCENTRATION CAMP IN THE NEIGHBORHOOD

A friend of mine, Ron Jackson, shared with me these words one evening. "Once God breaths breathe into you, He will show you who your neighbor is." You may be surprised that His view of who your neighbor is will be far beyond your limited understanding of just a house next door, but it well could be that you would be asked to expand your interest beyond even the borders of your country. Bernie and Victor, Tatiana and Elsa and Alba called out from across the seas. They became neighbors. Day to day living includes being a neighbor to our own families like getting over disappointments, grudges, hate and emotional stress caused by people who need forgiveness. There are a host of people whose memory banks need to be flushed. If we do not extend forgiveness it will become baggage that we will carry each day.

Who is my neighbor? They may be... politicians, morticians, skinheads, dead heads, tax evaders, street kids, alcoholics, blue collar and white collar workers, war mongers, peace nicks, suicidal, shut-ins, drop out, friendless, homeless, foreigners, aliens, Muslims, feminists, evolutionists, creationists, perverts, slum lords, Protestant, Catholics, pro-choice, pro-life, black, white, family, brother, sister, police, obese, lawyers, sex offenders, gays, lesbian, demagogues, preachers, doctors, judges or juries.

The ultimate example of all the places God allowed me to visit was a Concentration Camp in Poland. Hate reigned supreme. Belorussia and Bulgaria come in at a close second. All of the prisoners in this Camp were at one time residing in a neighborhood. All of the prison authorities were once residing in a neighborhood. But neighborhoods turned into a hate fest. Racism ran wild that eventually turned into a war. Hate is a hard task master.

Malcolm Eudaley

MAJDANEK CONCENTRATION CAMP – APRIL 1994

Minsk, Belorussia; Lublin, Poland and Warsaw, Poland

On a return trip from Moscow to the U.S. a small group of us went to Minsk, Belorussia for a short stop. Our contacts there were limited. Spending time in this place was depressing. There was not a moment in which one could feel comfortable and at ease.

Everything began with a slow, steady diet of manipulation and mind control. This is the way systems change. Eventually a country wakes up to the fate of a slow socialism that usually moves further with its intrusions until a population is consumed by such a fate.

Alexander Tyler wrote in the 1800's that 'Nations' progress through this sequences. "From bondage to spiritual truth to great courage; from courage to liberty, from liberty to abundance, from abundance to selfishness, from selfishness to complacency, from complacency to apathy, from apathy to dependence, from dependence to bondage."

At such a time the word 'Profit' becomes an evil word. The word 'fairness' surfaces; share the wealth. Such fairness ends up with the government in control. Belorussia is still one of the countries that are bent toward Communism. The oppression that exists in this place is seen in the faces of everyone. Bulgaria comes in second in this world of Communism and Socialism.

From Moscow we fly to Warsaw with plans to drive to the city of Lublin in Southern Poland. There is a University in this city where an American Professor is teaching. Terry Mitchell and his wife were serving through an agency that specialized in such placements. While with the Mitchell's we visited with a young adult student who was indeed on a quest to discover the Christian faith. Our conversation with him was limited. Our time together was concluded by praying the Lord's Prayer together.

Terry then suggested that we go to the nearby site of the Majdanek Concentration Camp. This camp opened in 1941 under the orders and control of Hitler. This was the year I graduated from high school. Little did this boy of eighteen ever dream of seeing such a place. During the time of its existence there would be over 300,000 prisoners held in this inhuman place. Most of these prisoners would be Jewish. Some would be Polish and Russian. Most of them died. They died in gas chambers, or ovens, by firing squads, cold weather, starvation or beatings. The mind goes into extreme bewilderment in such a place.

On November 3, 1943, a terrible event happened in this Camp. The Nazis called this event by the name of Erntefest, which means Harvest Festival. The prisoners called it 'bloody Wednesday.' Eighteen thousand Jews were executed. It was the largest mass killings carried out at any of the concentration camps in the history of the Holocaust. The victims were the last remnants of the Jewish population in Lublin and Warsaw.

At a point in time Typhus broke out. The results were that a large ditch was dug under the orders of the Camp Director. This ditch was very deep. Trucks were brought in to haul these prisoners from the barracks to this site. The S.S. came to serve as the Executioners.

The place has been preserved by the Polish government. Standing at this site is a Crematorium for the cremation of prisoners. The gas chambers were present and used to kill. Water showers would be turned on followed by the releasing of gas into the room. Later a mausoleum was built where these prisoners' ashes were placed along with small bones of the remains. There is a monument that was erected by the Polish government as a statement to mankind. A script was written and placed on the monument, making en eternal statement to we who live.

LET OUR FATE BE A WARNING TO YOU

To visit each of these sites was an astounding experience. To think, that man would do this to man. As we walked through each of these sites, more and more it seemed that such a place was inconceivable. This was reality. The reality of it was saying so much about the potential of and the existence of evil in the world. One can hardly sing 'Kum bye aye' in such a setting. Some would say that neither is God good all the time. I find it interesting that man could do such evil, yet blame God for what man has done to his own. History confirms that evil does exist in our world. Are we being surprised at what happens in our own cultures? Is there coming through a subtle 'side door effort' an introduction of Euthanasia into the Culture we live in?

Our return to Warsaw was a pleasant event after visiting this camp. The city had been rebuilt, at least somewhat to its old former image. The night before we flew back to American we attended a Concert conducted by a symphony orchestra. It was not a black tie event for us since we traveled in very functional attire. The evening was what we needed. It was like returning to civilization out of a world of madness.

GLOBAL EXPOSURE TO SOCIALISM

To me, it seems to be impossible to understand Socialism and Communism without experiencing these systems. One needs to be on site, rub shoulders with it, walking in the midst of it. Most causes or systems can be presented in theory or academically, yet not be proven in fact. The title for this book, "Come Walk the World," is no loose statement of a casual visit. Nor it is some shallow make believe experience. When you are deep in this kind of world, you will come to understand how it impacts the people who live in it 24/7. Mentally, physically and spiritually the end result is that such a system produces limitations on the people who live there. Some come to accept these limitations.

To be present in such a place – to experience exposure to it – causes it to become real in the worst sense of the word. That exposure took place for me in many settings: China, Cambodia, Romania, Bulgaria, Belorussia, Russia, the Ukraine and Poland. It was not a textbook walk, nor was it theory. It was something you sensed and smelled and understood.

The people who were leading us, believers in the Christian faith, were looking out for us. You did not talk freely in a restaurant. When one traveled by train it was necessary to be quiet. You were a foreigner and you knew it. A twelve-hour train trip at night from Kiev to the Western border of the Ukraine was hopefully a safe journey – especially since we purchased a compartment ticket. Yet one was not comfortable in this confinement situation. A cancelled trip from Isai, Romania to Odessa, Ukraine was necessary due to some uncertainty that came to our attention.

Life is very simple for these people. Villages and small towns were so poor. Farmers did not have adequate equipment for the fields. The diet consisted of potatoes, tomatoes, pork, and carp fish with little other food stuffs. Cucumbers were raised by the tons. Great farm lands were available in the old Soviet Union. If the Ukraine had possessed the farm equipment of the U.S. farmer, the lives of these folk could have been much better. It was the system that was destroying them. Horses and wagons were still being used. There were a few tractors, possibly fifty years old. Homes, cars, streets, poorly constructed high-rise apartments, the cross country train system were worn out. Make do furniture, undependable utilities and state schools for children that were poorly equipped were common. Orphanages warehoused children. Kiev and Moscow were blessed with a good underground subway system.

CHAPTER 9
THE FAR EAST

MALAYSIAN MOTHER MURDERED
FORGIVENESS OF A DAUGHTER

Three trips were made into this Region. We fly into Kuala Lumpur, the capitol of Malaysia. There we met with a Chinese brother, Enoch Tan. Enoch introduced us to a governmental official that lived north of the capitol. His wife was named Dorothy.

Their house was very large, but there were some inhabitants in a far away bedroom that we were to meet. David Showalter was traveling with me. This family fed us a good meal and took us to a far away bedroom that was not often used. We were sleeping on two twin mattresses lying on the floor. In the night David needed to get up. He turned on the lights and on every wall and on the ceiling all kinds of small animal. They had invaded the place. With the lights on, they ran in every direction possible. They were not bothering us, so we turned the light off and went back to sleep.

Something far more important was about to happen the next day.

Dorothy was a Chinese lady. Earlier in her life when she was ten or twelve year-old child, the Japanese had invaded Malaysia. Dorothy's mother was a very political active person in Malaysia. The Japanese discovered this and began to integrate her. The harassment became more difficult until eventually the Japanese sentenced her to death by a Firing Squad of soldiers.

The tragedy was to be compounded when the date was set for Dorothy's mother to be executed. The Japanese forced Dorothy to be present for this execution. The time was set and Dorothy watched the Japanese firing squad kill her Mother. For years Dorothy endured this pain. To hear her tell of this event was so difficult. She hated the Japanese. As she moved into her adult years after the war Japanese business men would come to Malaysia and meet with select companies to transact business. Dorothy worked for a Malaysian

Company that did business with the Japanese. When the Japanese would come to her office, she would struggle within herself, trying to cover the pain.

Later, Dorothy became a Christian in this land of idols and false religions. As she processed her faith, becoming stronger with each test, she experienced the joy of being able to forgive the people who killed her Mother. Jesus made a statement the day He was suffering on the Cross? "Forgive them." Remember, that was an act of murder also. But it was more than that. It was an act of redemption.

Regardless of the culture we live in – regardless of our nationality, the color of our skin, our lack of education, damaged emotions can be cured by the Christian Faith. Regardless of our being in church, or being out of church, wherever we are, whoever we are, the Christian faith will cure our damaged emotions. The mind and the soul can be transformed. Our Lord helps people overcome abuse, hate or violence and will lead to forgiveness. You may never be able to erase the hurt, nor is it necessary to re-establish a relationship, but you can forgive. He did. You can. How? – by encountering Christ, the Redeemer.

CHINA - THE POPULATION HUB OF THE WORLD

It was a privilege to make three trips into China. The first was a limited trip into Hong Kong for a few days when I was serving with World Vision International. The second was spent in Guangzhou for a teaching event with some pastors as well as some lay people. Our last trip was more extensive. This trip permitted us to accomplish more since we went into the interior of the country to the city of Dawan. On most of our journeys over the Globe some journaling took place. However, on this trip some extensive journaling was done. Today, I am sharing from my journal selective notes from over fifty pages.

We fly out of Los Angeles on Cathy Pacific airlines on September 17, 1996. Charles Baldwin is traveling with me into a jet stream that will cause us to be in the air fourteen and a half hours. We arrive in Hong Kong and spend the night.

Our Chinese Team from Malaysia arrived on the 19th in Guangzhou. The contact we had in Malaysia has organized a small group of business men who are active Christians. They were coming to China to network with us. The team members are Andrew and Joseph, and Charlie, a mechanical engineer, and Brother Lee. While waiting for the arrival of the team, Charles and I visit some sites in Guangzhou, especially the White Swan Hotel. It was one of the most beautiful hotels in the world. We had stayed a few blocks away in something like a Motel 6.

On Friday, the 20th, our rented van arrived and we take off for Dawan. The trip will take all day. Brother Cho, who resided in Dawan, arranged for Charles and me to rent two rooms at the Regional Communist Party Headquarters. Everybody likes to make money. The rooms were simple. They even had window air conditioners. The showers were ice cold.

A Chinese man by the name of Cho, had served as an agent of the communist party in Dawan. The Communist Committee had placed Cho in the local church as an undercover person. We would spend the week here in a Pastor training event. Cho began his assignment and after a period of time was converted to Christianity. The Party, to date, had not brought any charges against him.

The pastor training event was scheduled to begin on Monday, September 23rd. On Saturday, the 21st, we went on a tour of the country side. Our transportation was a Romanian one cylinder farm vehicle work horse. It was built like a tiller. We could not imagine this machine in this place. They had attached a small two wheel trailer for us to stand in. The ride consisted on each one holding on to the other.

Our first village to visit was named Ki-phong which means 'place where Chickens meet.'

We are taken to a church where the believers had gathered. About 100 people packed the building. These people were farmers and extremely poor. They asked Charles to speak. He talked to them about the man in the Bible named Barnabas.

When their church service was over we went outside. People gathered around asking us to have special prayers with them. I prayed with a man that was holding a three month old child who had a fever. The child's mother had died. At every turn we were asked to pray for the healing of people. In my journal I wrote: 'As a Christian, don't go to China if you do not believe in healing'.

Later on this Saturday, we go to visit Brother Cho's place in a small village. There is a clan of about 15 families of 130 people. Cho is considered to be a rich man. He has a four room house. Roasted peanuts and tea are served. He has a wife with four children. Photos were being taken. Enoch suggested that Mr. Cho pose with his wife for a photo and ask that he place his arm over her shoulder. He said, "He has never placed his arm around her shoulder in public."

As we left, looking back, Mrs. Cho is standing alone at the edge of her village. She was one of the loneliest persons I have ever seen. Enoch says, "The women of China are lonely people." She was troubled by his touch in public.

There were approximately 500 in attendance at the Sunday worship service. Their building was very large, but very poorly furnished. The seating was simple. The seats had no back to lean against. Their hymns were songs from the west – written out on the back of old calendars they had found. I spoke for the morning service. A translator can make you or break you. Possibly I was breaking myself.

At 7 am on Monday a group of about 30-40 people gathered for study and prayer. They meet 365 days a year. Their time together is usually for one hour. They close by singing "I have decided to Follow Jesus."

At 9:15 we begin the training class for pastors. This will be a week long event. Most of this group is made up of young men and women. Women in ministry in China are quite common. Charles will be teaching each day. There will be times when the class will break up into small groups. The subject matter is from the Sermon on the Mount. Charles, who has taught at the college level for about 25 years, does a wonderful job for the week.

On the closing day of this event the son of Brother Cho came from a distant city to visit his parents. This son could speak some limited English. In conversation over lunch it was discovered that the young man had not taken on a Christian name. Enoch spoke to Charles and suggested that he give Cho's son a name. Charles said, "My grandfather was named John and I have a son named. John." It was confirmed and the young man was given the name of John.

On the following Saturday we begin our return trip to Guangzhou. The Van Driver is driving to fast, using his horn to clear the road of people, water buffalo and cattle. A young calf is walking on the road and fails to move quickly enough. The Van is unable to miss this animal.

The Calf is struck by the side of the Van and falls in the road. The Driver keeps blowing the horn. He does not give a thought to stopping.

LEPER COLONY

In the same region of south-east Asia is the nation of Thailand. We fly to Bangkok. Our team spends a couple of days at the Presbyterian Mission Compound. While we were there, they invited us to visit a small leper colony outside the city. Traveling with us on this journey was our friend, Larry Dodd. At home in Iowa, Larry served as an evangelist who specialized in gospel music. When we entered the leper facility we did not know what to expect. The rooms were clean. The Lepers were clean. We simply went among them to visit. They were so warm to us. Then Larry began to sing to them. He would go about the room visiting with them, showing such kindness. Some would be seated on the floor and he would stoop down, hold their hand, and sing some great hymn. This event went on for some time – hymn after hymn. They began to cry. We began to cry. In the heart of most hymns there is great comfort as well as great Truth.

Malcolm Eudaley

You and I could have been born in Thailand, or Cambodia, or China. We could have experienced leprosy, but it did not happen. Through the amazing providence of God we were born in a land of wealth, with wonderful health care. But for the grace of God, not luck, we are here. Since this has happened to us, we are more the debtor to be a good neighbor in our world.

CHAPTER 10
LATIN AMERICA

After traveling east and west through the many time zones the Board of Global Education Plus transferred our activities into Central and South America region. The Caribbean also opened up for us in the Dominican Republic. A trip was scheduled to visit Guatemala. There we met in the offices of the Association of Christian School International. We were thankful for the opportunity they extended to us. We had networked with this Agency in Russia and the Ukraine. The Latin American office shared information related to a large number of schools in Central America as well as in South America.

Our purpose was to assist schools with textbooks, classroom equipment, building repairs as well as erecting new school houses. Some over the counter medicines, such as vitamins and de-worming pills, would be shared. We also had the privilege of visiting many of these schools. Some buildings would not qualify to be a good barn in our country. The lack of good books, maps, and classroom equipment were common at each of the schools visited. A plan was created to make visits and discover for ourselves the actual needs. What a time for us. We met some of the finest people serving these schools. We were shocked at the lack of everything a school needed to seeing them make do with what they had, and doing it successfully.

ELSA, A GREAT PRINCIPAL

Elsa represents the best of the best in a developing nation. When we first met her she was a 32-year-old widow. Her school, the Berea Christian School, was located in the highlands of rural Guatemala. She had 150 children enrolled. In the five years we have been involved with this school the classes have grown. The school board would met with us on our visits. They shared their financial records along with a report of the actions they were taking to give the school proper directions. As their financials were shared with us each of us commented that this little school had better records than some churches we knew.

Come Walk The World

Elsa's young husband had died 2 years prior to our meeting. His death was due to his having a brain tumor. The two of them had bought a simply little house in their village prior to his illness. Their home was setting on one lot with an adjoining empty lot next door. On our first visit she took our team to see her home. We had a simple meal with her.

On our second visit, a year later, we went to her home again. After visiting with her in this simple Guatemala home, she invited us to see her back yard. Five of us made up the Team. There she showed us the adjoining lot. A work crew was pouring footings for a new home. She had sold the land in order to pay her husband's medical bills. She gave a gift to her church and gave the remainder of these funds to her school. The five of us stood in amazement as she told this story. We were stunned. As we walked back to the school not much was said by anyone. On our arrival, standing at the edge of this school property, Dr. Chris Halvorson stopped and simply said, "Okay fellows it's time to empty your pockets." Our Agency had already given her a gift. This was the last of ten schools we had visited in the past five day. When we emptied our pockets we had $2,313 dollars to share with Elsa and her school children. The gift was given at the final meeting of the teachers and children in a chapel service.

The school board was present. They quickly showed us their budget needs to finish the second floor of a twelve room school they were building. The budget need was $2,307 dollars. Later they would complete the third floor of this masonry building.

For the past four years Global Education Plus has shared scholarship funds with Elsa in order for her to complete her college degree at a University in Guatemala City. Each Saturday morning at 4:30 am, she boards what I called a chicken bus to travel to the University. Many of you have seen such buses in other developing nations. These buses are packed with people, chickens, coffee beans, produce, kids along with Pedro and Maria. It was a three hour drive each way. Elsa will attend 4 classes with a break for a sack lunch she brought along. That evening she is back on the bus for the long ride home. She is now very close to completing her degree.

I suppose it will be very difficult for me to share the depth of a very spiritual relationship that evolves in such encounters. There are experiences that many of you have gone through that took on a higher level of friendship and admiration for another person. I think such an experience can happen when one is seeing another person who lives with a genuine core value system. A culture can be so cheap.

On the other side of the coin, life can bring on experiences that cause people to feel that they have been used. It may even be family. At such times one may feel cheated, burned out, from the stress and disappointment we have experienced. In working with hundreds of schools in Russia, the Ukraine along with Latin America we have only had two bad experiences. In one of these encounters my pastor, J. K. Warrick was traveling with us. When we returned to the van he said to us, "Mark this up to the reality of life. Not everything or everyone will be genuine."

Elsa is representative of several hundred teachers and principals who are great examples of living out their lives serving other people. Moving beyond Guatemala we found such people in Paraguay, Brazil, Honduras, Dominican Republic, Russia and the Ukraine.

TRANSFORMATION CAN HAPPEN ANYWHERE

In November of 2002 a team from Global Education Plus was scheduled to travel to

Guatemala on one of our annual trips. We arrived and were met by an ACSI representative. After an overnight stay in Guatemala City, we boarded our van and began a five day trip into the interior of Guatemala. The team would be visiting two schools a day. This trip would indeed be life changing for one of our travelers.

From the beginning of the trip we sensed a unity among us. We would be spending time in the van as well as eating our meals together. On this trip the van was full of singing. Normally, we would visit, talking about family, careers, the country we were in and its customs.

One of these travelers had been invited to be on the GEP Board from its inception. In creating this 501@ he asked me, after our second organization meeting, if I had invited him to serve on the board had a deeper purpose than his sharing gifts with the organization. I assured him that there were other motivations.

After five days of intense travel we were on our way back into Guatemala City. It was late but the singing was still taking place. Just before we arrived in Guatemala City our friend spoke up saying to us, "I do not know one thing about what it means to be a Christian." He said he was amazed by what he was experiencing on the trip. "I am very interested in becoming a Christian."

The group shared their stories of making such a commitment. We prayed with him. It was meal time so we stopped at a McDonald's as we entered Guatemala City. The team continued on to our hotel. He and I roomed together that night and I shared with him that everything would come together as he processed his confession and prayed to the Father. Significant things can happen without being in a church building.

We flew back to Kansas City arriving about sundown. I invited him to spend the night with us, but he chose to continue his journey to Minneapolis. He had flown to Kansas City to begin the trip in his private plane – a Mooney single engine aircraft. It was fully equipped with auto pilot. When the plane lifted from the runway of the Executive Airport in Olathe, Kansas, he reached his desired altitude, he put the plane on auto pilot. He then entered into an encounter with our Lord that brought about an amazing transformation in his life. The following is some of the content of a letter I received from him three days later.

"What an incredible experience we had in Guatemala. It was so intense that at times I remember thinking that this will all wear off in a few days after returning. Well, it hasn't. The return trip in my plane was a wonderful experience. I took off about sunset and flew in clear night air with a large moon shining into the cockpit. I took the opportunity to pray and reflect on the trip. Like all sinners, I felt that I had problems and complications that are almost unfixable – barriers between me and a close relationship with God that seemed insurmountable. I decided to put everything in God's hands. For years, I have believed that the Lord had a plan for me, but I have never had the courage to step forward and face it. But what I saw in Guatemala has helped me immeasurably. People there have nothing except faith and courage. How can a person like me, who has everything, refuse to draw on the same courage from God these people in Guatemala has." - Dean Baldwin

TEACHER TRAINING EVENTS DEVELOP – GUATEMALA, HONDURAS, PARAGUAY

After visiting so many schools in the world, Global Education Plus developed a "Preliminary Plan' to create One Week conferences for extension education purposes. Teachers who served these many Christian schools would be more effective through such a program. ACSI was the academic force in developing the format for such events, as well as the administration force.

We suggested these conferences be one week in length. We would fund food, lodging, teaching materials and meet some transportation needs. In some nations a teacher can teach in primary grades with a high school education. Others require some university training.

To date we have sponsored a total of five such events in Guatemala, Honduras and Paraguay. Each event has had approximately 30 teachers in attendance. Local professors from the nation's universities, who are comfortable with the Christian Worldview approach, come and serve at minimum cost. Other professors from the U.S. also come to teach. These schools are a great means of expanding the Christian faith as well as providing a good education for poor children in these nations. Each of these five events has been funded by Global Education Plus for $7,000 for a total of $35,000. GEP hopes to continue funding this training.

If the mission agencies of the world would have considered the development of a Christian school each time they established a church, the expansion of the Kingdom of God could have expanded with greater results. Not everything has to be developed in His world from a pulpit. The Kingdom is larger than we think. It can unfold through many different formats. It has.

A classroom could have an amazing variety of personalities present – possibly a Samuel, a David, a Timothy, even a Demas or a Judas. Maybe Ruth and Esther, Lois and Rachel, maybe even a Jezebel. It may be that you might not know some of these persons named above who once were kids. Their stories are in the Book. Who will succeed? Who will be mediocre, who will fail? Education can be a mighty tool. The youth a school presents to the public upon graduation can become a strong force for good, or a serious liability for a culture. Such a risk will not be determined by us.

WORLD NEWS

UNICEF states there are more than one billion children in poverty throughout the earth. Thirty per cent of these children in the developing world are not in school. Nine hundred million people are living in slums. Some of the ACSI schools are located in these slums. Few of these children will be able to enroll in any school. Few will hear the Good News. There will be no stained glass windows for them to view, or a 'power point' presentation. No 'hot' 'ready mix band' making music to the beat of a loud drummer in a sanctuary will be heard by them, nor will they encounter the Man from Galilee. Their chances are slim.

CHAPTER 11
GLOBAL EXPOSURE IN THE WEST

In a current best seller entitled "John Adams", written by David McCullough, Abigail Adams, wife to John, writes to her husband while he was attending the Continental Congress. She is quoting William Shakespeare.

"There is a tide in the affairs of men, which, taken at the flood, leads on to fortune, omitted, all the voyage of their life is bound in the shallows of miseries. We must take the current when it serves, or lose our ventures."

This nation, your nation, came into being through great conflict; first, in the Continental Congress and second, on the battlefield. Strong engagement of 'mind' and 'musket' were used in order to liberate us from the evil empire of that day.

It is likewise for us. We will either engage in living or we will fall into obscurity. We will either find an amazing life to commit to or we will do our walking along the seashore, where waves will wash away our foot prints. You may possess great talent as well as a high intelligence and yet fail to find your place in life. There are countless numbers of people who have degrees, but have never found their place in life. As a boy on the Gulf Coast of Texas I remember going to the beach to walk with the sand fiddlers – a little crab-like creature that lives on the beach. They run in all directions, left, right, up, and down but never go anywhere.

For decades in the west we have placed the emphasis on the wrong idea. We have allowed a materialistic culture to spoon feed us a lie. Our dreams were, "If we could only improve the socioeconomic situation of people, then everything will be okay – People through such achievements would be happy." Victor Frankl in his book, *The Unheard Cry for Meaning,* says, 'the struggle for survival has subsided in the west, now the question has emerged – survival for what'? People today can have the means to live, but no meaning to live for. It could be; if we continue our drift toward a kind of socialism, we might never recover as a nation.

Frankl lived through a concentration camp experience in WWII, surviving the ordeal. In 9 days he dictated his book, *Man's Search for Meaning*. It sold 9 million copies. I chose to listen to such a man rather than the gurus who think that everything can be corrected by an economic recovery or by a revision of truth that has surfaced with strong backing from the post-modern thinking of today.

We are pushing for more sales and stroking our ego to save an economy that is packed with greed and contempt for integrity. Our governments is experiencing the same if not more so. Probably one third of the items America spends its money on are not a rational use of money. Money is being printed by the ton. As General Motors goes, so goes the nation. As I write, General Motors and Chrysler are considering bankruptcy.

Tony Blankley, a former PBS new commentator and writer says in his book, *The West Last Chance,* "of a possible introduction of a democratic and economic opportunity in the middle east that may surface, bringing peace and prosperity in these lands. They already have oil and wealth. They do not have peace; nor is there any sign of peace in the whole region.

Thomas L. Friedman in his book, H*ot Flat and Crowded*, says that "America has a problem – it has lost its way in recent years. The World has a problem. It is getting hot, flat and crowded – we need a course correction – we're on the wrong track. If we want to maintain our technological, economic and 'moral leadership'; things will have to change." So if we create a better technological and a better economic system along with a new 'moral leadership' we will have continuing peace and prosperity. I wonder what he means by calling for a 'Moral Leadership'. Who will lead this phase of the recovery, since greed and contempt for integrity is so lacking in leadership. A prominent Newsman for a major Network covered the bases for us by once stating, "It's all about sincerity, and if one can fake that, one has it made". There is much faking going on in the culture.

The North American Church has its own set of circumstances to contend with as it searches for meaning. T. David Gordon, former professor at Gordon-Conwell Seminary and author of 'Why Johnny Cant Preach' suggested we are becoming a 'cult of the insignificant.' He writes that our culture has ministers who are not at home with what is significant. In his book that was published in 2009, he convincingly states that three matters are not to be passed over;

- The great seriousness of the reality of being human
- The dreadful seriousness of the coming judgment of God
- And the sheer insignificance of the present in the light of eternity.

In the evolution of the Christian Faith, it appears that it is inevitable that man will always make an effort to bring about unnecessary change. The Communist brought on such change until the core of the Christian faith was stifled in their culture. Such a death can also happen by being passé to reality.

David Wells in his 2008 book *The Courage to be Protestant* shares in detail what is happening in the American church. 'The American personality is being built around the idea that nothing is fixed in life. Nothing is authoritative, and nothing absolute. There is no certainty of belief, behavior or values. The self becomes the authoritative force. Nothing can act as a norm. Political correctness is the solution. When Christ addresses the hypocrisy of men who appear so religiously incorrect, he is being judgmental. When the church says "We know," it is acting out of arrogance'.

It is true that some things have been overstated, but we do not throw the baby out with the wash because some one speaks out of a shallow mind. I heard a lady leaving the doctor's office at Easter time recently saying to the receptionist, "I hope the Easter Bunny is good to you this year." How serious she was I don't know. A substitute bunny is quite irrelevant when compared to the offer of eternal life by the Power of the Resurrection.

THREE WORLD'S MEET

Let's walk through three more events that bring us to the heart of the issue of what is true and significant alongside what is false and insignificant. It was our privilege to see throughout the old Soviet Union many statues of Lenin. In some cities of this world the people destroyed some of these statues. In other, his statue continues to stand as a representative of a failed system. In the city that I came to love, Lenin still 'stands' in a prominent location in downtown Kiev. Solzhenitsyn 'stood' at Harvard as a clear voice. Jesus 'stood' in Jerusalem and identified himself as the Way, the Truth and the Life. Lenin was never a convincing voice standing for Truth.

In 2008, Charles Colson, in Christianity Today writes of an address given by Solzhenitsyn at Harvard University. It was the 327th commencement at Harvard. He writes of "the abandonment of its Christian heritage with all the moral horrors that followed. Man has become the master of this world; who bears no evil within himself; so all the defects of life are attributed to wrong social systems. Fashionable trends evolve with people being hemmed in by the idols of the prevailing fad. He even predicted Americans would care more about the rights of 'Terrorists' than stand against their evil deeds. This oppressed intellectual even offered to the faculty of Harvard and the graduating class, a solution – "A spiritual blaze is needed to recover our footing."

MOSCOW AND LENIN

While on one of our trips into Moscow we were walking through Red Square. Plans were made to enter the building where Lenin resides. He is in a mausoleum under glass, airtight, with proper lighting. It is an eerie place. No words were spoken by the viewers. The security is also air tight. A person carrying a newspaper made a little noise. It was stopped immediately.

Here he lies. His legacy represents a bloody revolution of killing. Stalin is inspired by him. Lenin represents bondage, death, despair, deceit. A nation lies in ruin. He was a practicing atheist with no place for God.

The Russian are a great people who have been robbed of everything. Their dignity as a people has been crushed by an oppressive system of manipulation and control. After seeing Lenin we went next door to an Orthodox Cathedral just off of Red Square. One door was open to tourists. Other doors had chains to secure their entrances. Beautiful art work was in this cathedral for viewing. In one of the Onion Domes, I looked up to see a great work of art. It was a painting of the face of Christ. From any direction He was looking at you. Yet, His being there was meaningless to communists who controlled this world. To them it was only art.

JESUS AND JERUSALEM

On another trip our journey took us to another tomb. It is in Jerusalem. Visiting this tomb gives you a fresh perception of life. It is not a Mausoleum. It is a place of celebration. In this tomb the man Jesus Christ, lay less than 72 hours. Out of this tomb He arose, to change the world. Every event shared with you in this Global Exposure trip; all of the people we have written about had met this powerful resurrected One. His love flows throughout the whole earth today since He is alive. Rejoice in the Lord! Yes, we had a Good Friday with its death and suffering, but we also have an Easter Morning! I am writing this to you on Easter Sunday 2009.

REMEMBER
IT IS NOT PROPER THAT WE CHRISTIANS SHOULD RESIDE IN A MAUSOLEUM FOREVER

Disturb Us.
Disturb us, Lord, when
We are too well pleased with ourselves,
When our dreams have come true
Because we have dreamed too little,
When we arrived safely
Because we sailed to close to the shore.

Disturb, us, Lord when
With the abundance of things we possess
We have lost our thirst
For the Waters of life;
Having fallen in love with life,
We have ceased to dream of eternity

And in our efforts to build a new earth,
We have allowed our vision
Of the new heaven to dim.

Disturb us Lord, to dare more boldly,
To venture on wider seas
Where storms will show your mastery;
Where losing sight of land,
We shall find the stars.

We ask you to push back
The horizons of our hope;
And to push us into the future
In strength, courage, hope and love

-Sir Francis Drake - 1577

THE LAST SHALL BE FIRST

Two, possibly three times, this thought has surfaced as I have shared with you. The phrase is "The first shall be the last and the last shall be the first." On the surface such a comment seems preposterous. How can something be out front so far that no one would give any thought to it slipping into last place. Sir Francis Drake in his poem *Disturb Us* implies that one can become so enamored with the accomplishment of his dreams coming true that he relaxes and decides to sail to close to the shore line.

May 2, 2009, I watched on TV the Kentucky Derby in Louisville. I have no interest in betting or wining on a horse race. My interest comes from a love I have for one of the most graceful animals on earth. There are others, such as seeing a well trained bird dog with a covey of quail, or some beautiful peacocks strutting about with their tails unfolded. I have never owned a horse. As a young boy living in south Texas I almost had one in my possession. The year was 1930. In that part of Texas the cattlemen, as well as those who owned horses, had what was called 'open range.' There were no fences across the prairies. A little colt strayed into our little town one day. This colt seemed to be sick. A group of us boys decided to play Veterinarian. We put together a concoction of things like vinegar, catsup, water, etc. After pouring this mix down the colt's throat, he decided his life was in danger and if he was going to live, he needed to get away from these experts on horse survival. My ownership hopes faded as he ran off into the sunset, returning to the prairie.

Such a horse arrived at the 2009 Kentucky Derby. He did have a good blood line, but absolutely no reputation. A cowboy, along with some friends, had purchased him for $9,500. The stables at the Derby were filled with "million dollar" horses. Horses had even been flown in from the nation of Dubai. The trainer of "Mine That Bird", Bennie Woolley, Jr., had brought his horse to Louisville in a trailer pulled by a pick-up truck. It had taken him 21 hours to drive from New Mexico. A toothless jockey by the name of Calvin Borel would take this so-called scrub of a horse to the starting gate. Underneath the skin of 'Mine that Bird" was a determined thoroughbred. The odds on his winning were 50 to 1. In a horse race those odds are as bad as it gets.

There were 153,563 in attendance at the Derby. The rich and the famous gathered with the expectation of seeing one of the horses from a major stable from America or Dubai take home the purse and the roses. The Derby is also a style show for women who attend. The hats worn by these ladies were large and extremely colorful. It was a money place. The only little people present were the stable boys along with the trainer Bennie Woolley, Jr. He was so out of his league, it appeared. He simply did not belong at the

Derby. His horse did not belong at the Derby. Bennie had worked on the rodeo circuit. He rode motorcycles and arrived at the Derby on crutches. He had broken his leg riding a motorcycle. The Derby is a class act. "Mine That Bird" at 50 to 1 odds should have been entered into a dog and pony show race being held at some small county fair grounds event. But, in spite of all that was against Bennie, he went to the Derby and WON! He was supposed to come in last! In fact, he did come out of the gates at Churchill Downs last, stumbling. It was to be his day. What a surprise.

    Surprises have always been around.
David, the Shepherd boy took a sling shot
    and WON a battle against a giant.
    His brothers knew he would lose.
The three Hebrew boys had no chance in a
    fiery furnace,
but they had a special Guest appear and
    WON.
Esther was doomed to die, but a surprise
    took place.
Jesus rode into Jerusalem on a Colt, with all
    of the odds against him.
    He WON the race!

Paul, on board a ship for Rome is caught in a storm. The ship sinks.
He is rescued and later writes a major part of the New Testament.
It is never as it appears to be.
You can win against all Odds.

CAST OFF THE LINES

'Cast off the lines,' or 'lift the anchors,' were common terms aboard our ship. The executive officer would give the order to men on the docks. When we were in port in the U.S. there would be a tug boat to assist in our leaving dock. Overseas, when we would not have a tug boat to assist, the Captain would have to maneuver the ship away from the dock through orders to the engine room and the man at the wheel who controlled the rudder. Before anything can happen that allows a ship or a boat to move out onto the water, some one has to cast off the lines.

I met some men one time who decided to go fishing. They had experienced something very unusual a few days before. They had met a man who had died, but in some mysterious way had returned to life. They were not sure what to think or what to do. So the leader of the group suggested that they return to what they had been doing before they met this amazing man. The seven of them go back to a familiar seaside where they had fished before. "Let's go fishing." When they arrived at the shore line they found the old boat they had used in the pasts for fishing. Possibly it had been tied to a little dock or maybe it was just resting on the beach.

They cast off the lines and proceeded to fish all night. They caught nothing. Some times when we are confronted with reality we resolve our confusion by simply returning to the humdrum of a dull, unproductive life. Life is more than you or me entering into a task that only provides for the hunger of the body and a roof over our head. Our task, our work is important in providing materials things, but there is something more.

When the sun came up, there is a lone figure standing on the beach. He shouts to the seven. "Good Morning. Did you catch anything for breakfast?" "No," they call back. The man on the beach calls out "Throw the net off the right side of the boat and see what happens." They did and their nets filled with fish.

The man on the beach is very interested in you as well as others in being productive. But, he has something more to say to the seven. He has something to say to us. When they arrive on the beach there is a fire burning with fish and bread cooking. "Bring some of the fish you've just caught." No one says a word. They now know that this is the man who died in Jerusalem and has returned to Life.

As they are eating, He asked the leader some questions. The remaining six men are standing near the fire. They are listening as this amazing man ask, "Simon, son of John do you love me more than these? Three times this question is asked of Peter. The questions may not seem to be the right ones to ask a grown man, but deep within the question there is to be found the most important matter that any person will ever be asked in his/her lifetime. "Do you love me?" All of these disciples would joint with Peter, casting off the lines of the old life.

AT THE EDGE OF THE WORLD

Wherever people live, you will find men and women like Pastor Kushnir in the Ukraine; Bernie in the Philippines; Baranbas, in Cambodia; Tatiana, in Russia; Elsa, in Guatemala; Jorge and Stuart in Guatemala; Esteban in Paraguay; Sophia, in Taiwan; Daniel, David and Nicolae in Romania; Juriy, in Chernovsty, Ukraine; along with Viktor in Odessa and Pastor Kaminchi of Korsten Ukraine. Each of these men and women were asked the question, "Do you love me?" They each answered in the affirmative, "Yes, Lord." Each of them responded to an assignment designed just for them. They are rich and productive. They are persons who are happy and contented, having searched for meaning and found it. To the best of my knowledge they are all alive. They have cast off the lines and moved out onto the seas of discipleship and service; having a clear understanding of what it is to have a Christian Worldview of life. They are moving forward in reality.

Today, we reside in a very discontented world, east and west, north and south.
Much of Europe is in disarray having embraced socialism.
England has become a multi-cultural morass. Muslims may well become the dominant force on the continent and England.
The Arch Bishop of Canterbury, so well educated, is confused.

The American Church seems to be uncertain of its roots, struggling with belief and behavior.
An important question arises: "Do we understand the times?"
Strange as it may be China Christians have a dream to spread Christianity.
Latin America is alive with a strong evangelical base.
African churches are rejecting the Church of England.
Change is the theme of the day in D.C., but to what?
There is one leader who has not changed. He is the same.

THE MESSAGE IS STILL ALIVE

There are church and mission agencies that have not lost the vision. There are large groups and small groups who continue to spread the Good News. Some U.S. ministries and churches are lagging behind developing nations in their growth. In many places of the world the Spirit of the Lord is moving. There exist in the world small and large pockets of believers who still have a dream and a solution. The amazing truth of the Kingdom of God is that it will never die. Have there been failures? Yes, but there have been many successes.

In January 2009 Global Education Plus was approached by a young couple living in China. They have lived in this nation for twelve years. Their ministry has been varied and challenging. For the past four years Kyle and Lara Schwendemann have been working with the Hui people – the Box People. The majority are Muslim. Kyle and Lara have developed a relationship with an elementary school that is providing space for them to open a new start school. In another arena, two small groups of these folk are meeting. Baptizing has taken place. GEP has begun a networking experience with this young couple. This is a great investment opportunity. The returns on this investment will be deposited in a more secure bank. Hopefully our efforts will expand to this young couple who has moved beyond the passion of secular achievement.

COME WALK THE WORLD

However you may view life, if someone sends you a beautiful Embossed Invitation to a very special event, usually you would at least read it. That is what I have attempted with you, the reader. We began with a sweeping invitation to you - Come Walk the World . I asked you to read this story from the first paragraph that told of a funeral in Khadbarovsk, Northeast Russia to the end of the story of a young couple living with their two children in China.

We have crossed the Atlantic and the Pacific several times - gone to Alaska as well as Mexico, Central America, the Caribbean and South America. Most of these trips were to visit children going to school as well as the many adults who are investing their lives in these schools. Some amazing people have been visited.

All of these journeys have been made with a purpose. First, to share honor and respect to these great leaders who are unknown to the world. GEP also, gave support to their schools and other activities. I am thoroughly convinced that the 'first shall be last' after all of these journeys. Secondly, I have written from my heart in sharing their stories. These people have been impacted by the Lord. Their work would not continue without their discovering a reality – a reason for living and making a commitment to their discovery.

Face to face these people have challenged me. What was this all about? Why make these long, tiring trips to places few people have ever heard of, to meet with the so-called little people of the world? There were reasons. We live in a culture that has made many things quite cheap that are very valuable. Our culture has made the significant, insignificant.

It is good for one to be challenged. I have been challenged even in writing this book. I also write for You. Persons are of great worth and we all need to be challenged. There is no intent for me to Challenge you to do what I have done. That would be foolish. But your life is just as unique as mine or anyone else. You are of great value. Your life was designed to be creative, not destructive.

Brennan Manning in his book entitled *The Signature of Jesus* shares some comments on the courage to risk. "In pensive moments I wonder if I have the courage to risk everything for the Christian life. Is my service only make believe, still in bondage to the insecurity that wears a thousand masks, still thrashing about trying to fix myself, struggling for that elusive achievement that will make me presentable to the God of the Universe? Do we like to stay close enough to the fire to keep warm and be satisfied with the narrow dimensions of our partial commitment? Winston Churchill stated 'Success is never final; failure is never fatal. It is courage that counts."

TAKE THE STEP

I encourage you to give a moment to reflect on your engagement with life. The challenge to be faithful could come to you in a very unpredictable way. You will need to make a step that will cost you something. Every person sooner or later will face his/her own Cross; or, if you prefer, his/her own 'Waterloo'. Remember the seed of wheat must die before it can grow from the soil and be used to make bread. If you are already engaged in a significant matter for you, consider being a person who would wisely challenge and encourage someone else who is discouraged or dysfunctional, broken, defeated, and living without a purpose or plan for their lives.

When we walk into our crucible of fire, like the prisoners at Majdanek Concentration Camp, as well as the many persecuted leaders we have written about, we should already be acquainted with the Lord's Prayer. Their suffering brought out a kind of dignity that can only be discovered in the truth found in the Christian Faith. Such persons were dignified by the indignity; suffering shame and exposed to disgrace for His name. Yet, they remained true and continued speaking to their world and ours. How did they accomplish this? They rose above the systems they live in. We will rise above the disappointments and the failures in life when we move forward into "A Journey of Reality" and begin to pray; not through a formality, or simply from 'memory', but because we have come to know the FATHER.

Our Father who is in Heaven, hallowed by Thy name,
Your Kingdom come, your will be done on earth as it is in heaven. Give us today our daily bread.
Forgive us our trespasses
as we also forgive those who trespass against us.
And lead us not into temptation – (save us from ourselves)
And deliver us from the Evil one. Amen
(NIV) and (The Message)

GO... AND HAVE A GOOD LIFE

LaVergne, TN USA
23 December 2009
167904LV00001B/4/P